ANNUALS

Antique Flowers

ANNUALS

Yearly Classics for the Contemporary Garden

ROB PROCTOR

PHOTOGRAPHS BY ROB GRAY

WATERCOLORS AND SUPPLEMENTAL
PHOTOGRAPHS BY THE AUTHOR

FOREWORD BY HENRY MITCHELL

HarperCollins*Publishers*

FOR
BETTY MARIE

My big sister's drawing of a Sunflower inspired me at an early age to pick up both the paintbrush and the trowel.
Now she sends me sketches and beribboned packets of seeds—Sweet Williams and Black-eyed Susans—from her garden half a
continent away. Flowers, art, and siblings—how intertwined are the elements that have led to this book.

ANNUALS was conceived and produced by
Running Heads Incorporated
55 West 21 Street
New York, NY 10010

FIRST EDITION

Editor: Charles A. de Kay
Designer: Jan Melchior
Managing Editor: Lindsey Crittenden
Production Manager: Linda Winters

ISBN 0-06-016314-3
Library of Congress Catalog Card Number: 90-55549
Library of Congress Cataloging-in-Publication information is available.

Typeset by Trufont Typographers, Inc.
Color separations by Hong Kong Scanner Craft Co., Ltd.
Printed and bound in Singapore by Times Offset Pte. Ltd.

91 92 93 94 95 10 9 8 7 6 5 4 3 2 1

ACKNOWLEDGMENTS

As gardeners, we visit other gardens for various reasons: we learn, we measure the merits of our own gardens, we celebrate the accomplishments of other gardeners, and we envy them. Rob Gray's photographs document the triumphs of a number of accomplished gardeners. To the gracious people who opened their homes and gardens to us, we offer our thanks, tinged with just a bit of envy. We are also grateful to many people for their special contributions, including the floral designers who shared their special magic with flowers.

Ruth Koch
Bea Taplin
Anne Weckbaugh
Tweet Kimball
Sheilagh Malo
Sandy Snyder
Diane Dalton
The Honorable Governor of Colorado
 and Mrs. Roy Romer
Rosemary Verey
Margaret Fuller
Tom Peace
Karen and Jim Esquibel
Mary Kay Long and Dennis Unites
Nancy Brittingham
Nancy Stimson Watters
Allen Haskell
Lewis Hart
Beth Chatto
Jeanne Ruggles
Patricia Thorpe

Peter Stephens
Chris Lennon
Rennie Reynolds
Graymoor Antiques
Denver Botanic Gardens
Nyman's Garden
The Molly Brown House
Brooklyn Botanic Gardens
Strawbery Banke
The Washington Street Eatery
The Fuller Garden
Roseland Cottage
Old Sturbridge Village
Blackberry River Inn
Freund's Farm Market

Special thanks to:

Panayoti Kelaidis
Deane Hall

Ray Daugherty
Robin Preston
Angela Overy
Nancy Varney
Pat Hayward
Rita Buchanan
Solange Gignac of The Helen Fowler
 Library, Denver Botanic Gardens
Pat Pachuta
Nancy Ballek MacKinnon,
 Ballek's Garden Center
Starr Tapp
Thornton's Antiques
Susan Sheridan
Lin Hulbert
Kathy Meyer
Lianne Meyer
Edward Connors
Lauren Springer
Annie Duncan

CONTENTS

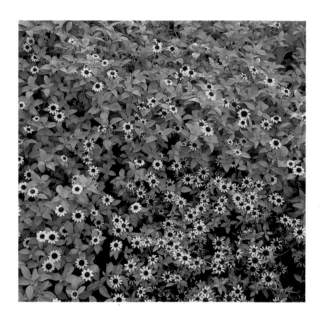

CHAPTER FOUR

A Portfolio
of Antique Annuals • 4 7

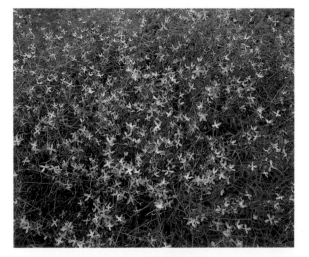

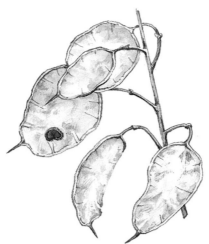

IT'S HIGH TIME ANNUALS
stopped apologizing to the rose, the acanthus, and the lily for daring to live in the same garden; and this renewed respect of flowers that sprout, flower, and die all in one year is a wholesome trend.

No doubt it is part of the general liberation movement detectable throughout the world, in which the humble and oppressed seek a place in the sun. And nowhere is the trend more timely than in gardens.

It had gotten to the point that a gardener almost automatically apologized for harboring a cosmos, and I know places where the presence of a cleome—that gorgeous and generous native—produced a polite silence with averted eyes from every visitor, as if the gardener had an unfortunate skin rash that had to be carefully ignored.

But however fierce the prejudice in favor of perennials has been, there are now and always have been gardeners less keen for transient fashion than for the chief sweet flowers, and now, fragrant or not, the old-fashioned annuals are coming back, even in the gardens of snobs.

FOREWORD BY
HENRY MITCHELL

I think it is all right to have nasturtiums spilling out on the garden paths once again. I hope so, as I have never given them up and never intend to.

You may wonder, as I do, which of the readers of this brisk, useful, and authoritative book will go out after sundown to check on the nasturtiums to see them emitting electric sparks. The author (who relays this hitherto unreported phenomenon without vouching for it) says it was observed in the eighteenth century in the household of the great Linnaeus himself. Man and boy I have grown nasturtiums more than sixty years and have never seen anything shoot off a nasturtium beyond an occasional wind-blown bug, but we should never be too old to investigate further.

Even in the daylight a radiance as magical as anything electrical may be seen in the common larkspur, cornflower, Sweet William, or dozens of other well-loved old flowers. However greatly neglected in re-

cent years in the gardens of fashion, the beauty of those old favorites has sustained them in all gardens of true flower-lovers.

Some flowers in this book are more familiar than others, and the sane steady gardener will wish to try many that are new to him. There are others, not exactly unknown but often passed over year by year, such as the tithonia. I never knew anybody who grew it even once who didn't think it glorious. And it grows as easily as a sunflower or a zinnia, yet I know of no other flower that gives off the same brilliance in its color range between orange and red.

One thing that has been lacking is a book in which particular annuals are discussed, not simply listed. Here they are treated, as they should be, as fully worthy of respectful and lively commentary as any rhododendron from the Himalayas.

To some readers this book will be a comfort; to others an inspiration; and to yet others a door to an expanded world of gardening. While especially valuable for those with small gardens, there is no reason a very grand person with grand acres should not enjoy it too.

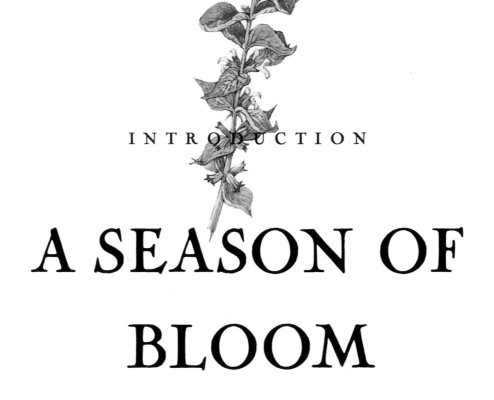

INTRODUCTION

A SEASON OF BLOOM

IF THERE IS A FLOWER WITH INDIVIDUALITY
AND A SET OF DELICATE SINGLE PETALS, THE
HORTICULTURALISTS SEEM DETERMINED TO
DOUBLE OR TRIPLE THEM, TO CURL THEM,
RUFFLE THEM, AND, INEVITABLY, TO MAKE
THEM BIGGER. THE RESULT IS THAT IN MANY
PAGES OF THE SEED CATALOGUES ALL BLOS-
SOM FORM SEEMS TO BE DISAPPEARING, CAUS-
ING ONE TO LOOK FEARFULLY AHEAD TO THE
TIME WHEN OUR GARDEN BEDS WILL BE FULL
OF GREAT, SHAGGY HEADS, ALIKE EXCEPT FOR
COLOR, ALL JUST GREAT BLOBS OF BLOOM.

—Katherine S. White , **Onward and Upward in the Garden**

THE FLOWERS THAT COMPLETE their life cycle in a single season are called annuals. The category is a large one, since many tender perennials that are not cold hardy are often grown as annuals. Biennials, which are confusing to some gardeners—for good reason—take two years to complete their life cycle. Some then proceed to confound the gardener by refusing to die, and then become known as short-lived perennials. (Some think that biennials are plants that bloom every other year—there is no such thing, to my knowledge, although my forsythia comes close.) Many of our so-called annuals are perennials in their native, usually tropical or sub-tropical, lands. Which plants are truly annual depends on the gardens in which they are grown.

This book of antique annuals (flowers that have been cultivated for at least one hundred years) includes plants generally considered to be annual or biennial in temperate climates. They are also, incidentally, representative of the many "unimproved" species that are beginning to be demanded by many gardeners. The desire to grow antique flowers is, in some respects, a rebellion against the creations of hybridists who have "improved" some flowers almost beyond recognition.

The mission of every annual is to bloom profusely, the better to entice insects to pollinate it, or allow the wind to do the job, and set prodigious amounts of seed to ensure the survival of the species. No energy is saved to be returned to the roots, as perennial plants do to survive the winter, and all systems are dedicated to flower and seed production. Gardeners have learned to frustrate their annual plants, re-

moving spent flowers before seed is produced in a process often called deadheading. This tricks the plants into producing flowers throughout the season. Pansies and petunias benefit from this treatment. Other plants don't require such treatment to bloom continuously—Sweet Alyssum and California Poppy come to

mind here—but are often sheared back in midsummer to rejuvenate them. Modern hybridists have bred sterile strains, commonly known as mules, that don't produce seed. It is estimated that over fifty percent of an annual's weight at season's end is in seeds. The decorative value of seed pods, both in the garden and for arrangements,

the high Victorian period, no matter the current calendar date. It has been said that nature abhors a straight line, but the Victorians, who were in the process of redrawing the lines of society as a whole, designed their gardens with geometric precision. The ribbon bed, rows of uniform bright annuals raised in the greenhouse and planted in lines, is a legacy of an age of affluence and affectation.

When the style had run its course, as it was bound to by economic considerations, as well as artistic ones, many annuals were shunned by the fashion revolution which swept carpet bedding out of the garden. The perennial border, as planted by purists, nearly forbade the inclusion of any annual flowers. Ironically, Gertrude Jekyll, who almost single-handedly replanted the beds of the Western world with perennials, loved annuals and included many annuals and tender perennials in her famous designs. Sweet peas, marigolds, stocks, and lavatera were given prominent roles in Jekyll borders.

Her decisions were based on color, form, and texture alone, and she looked at flowers with a fresh perspective, disregarding conventional placement and uses in other gardens. She had her prejudices too—she was not overly fond of most petunias—but her unique perspective allowed her to look beyond the use and misuse of annuals in the flower beds of late Victorian days. A valuable annual "should not be neglected because it is so common and so easy to grow and because it was so much overdone in monotonous lines in the old bedding days. Many good plants have of late suffered from a kind of mistaken prejudice on this account. But it should be

is often overlooked. Poppies, nigella, and lunaria have lovely pods.

The lion's share of credit for popularizing the annual belongs to the Victorians. That infamous trio of scarlet geranium, blue lobelia, and white alyssum, or variations thereof—so often copied without thought—can be considered a planting of

A garden, OPPOSITE, offers a kaleidoscope of annuals—*Chrysanthemum carinatum*, petunias, and salvias. ABOVE, Dahlberg Daisy fronts hybrid impatiens. BELOW, Gloriosa Daisy and pink phlox are handsomely paired.

remembered that if the plant was misused it was not the fault of the plant but that of the general acceptance of a poor type of gardening."

The purists, who adopted the perennial border as gospel, were not so forgiving. This narrow doctrine of "perennial only" provides an enormous challenge to the gardener: how to provide an entire season of color. There are glorious examples of triumph in this respect, but the genius to produce a continuously-blooming perennial planting is the most difficult feat in gardening, often beyond the scope of the mere mortal gardener. The results are often spotty, at best, and one or two months of glory (usually June) are followed by very little else. The gardener must use every trick at his disposal to manage a pretty garden in every season. Annuals are, indeed, the trick.

Those who insist on perennial-only schemes are also missing some of the most enchanting blooms the garden has to offer, not to mention a great deal of fun. Some voices insist that the goal of achieving flowers throughout the gardening season is not necessarily a good one, and that we would do well to concentrate instead on the diversity of plant form and leaf texture. One suspects they might have been less than successful in managing a border—name one gardener who started growing plants because they liked the shapes of the leaves. In time we learn to appreciate and value every aspect of plants as we cultivate them, and to plant them to best advantage, but it is the sly face of a pansy or the crinkled petals of a poppy that we first loved.

It is to the credit of modern gardeners

that annuals are now included in gardens in bold new ways, or in charming old-fashioned ones. Some choose to re-create or reinterpret the best of elaborate Victorian displays for period gardens, or to echo the unaffected abandon of the English cottage garden. The plantings vary from re-

The exuberance of a late summer garden, OPPOSITE, stems from prolific blooming *Cosmos bipinnatus* and *Cleome hassleriana*. Night-scented Stock, *Matthiola bicornis*, ABOVE, is edged with *Nierembergia caerulea*.

gion to region, but the new cottage garden encircles not only the genuine article in England, but also the adobe pueblos of Taos, the stuccoed bungalows of Miami, the shingled saltboxes of the Northeast, the rustic cabins of Minnesota, and the clapboard farmhouses of the Midwest.

Cascades of *Vinca major*, *Lobelia erinus*, and Dusty Miller, *Senecio cineraria*,
trail from a pedestal planter, ABOVE. The quintessential cottage garden flower, Foxglove,
Digitalis purpurea, RIGHT, has inspired folktales from time immemorial.

CHAPTER ONE

A HISTORICAL
PERSPECTIVE

GIVE ME THE GOOD OLD WEEKDAY BLOSSOMS

I USED TO SEE SO LONG AGO,

WITH HEARTY SWEETNESS IN THEIR BOSOMS,

READY AND GLAD TO BUD AND BLOW.

poet unknown

ANNUAL FLOWERS WERE NOT important features of Western gardens—those in Europe and America—until comparatively recent days. Those with healing or culinary uses, like Dill and Borage, were grown in medieval cloisters. Growing flowers for beauty alone came with the Renaissance, and the flower garden as we

know it evolved in the early seventeenth century in England. Perennials and shrubs of Britain and the European continent were predominant, and the native annuals, charming as they may appear to our eyes, weren't thought to be terribly showy and were largely ignored. As explorers ventured to new worlds, and European countries laid the foundations for empires, new plants, both annual and perennial, found favor in the garden. Crusaders are thought to have brought seeds of hollyhocks to England. Spanish missionaries sent seeds of nasturtiums, four o'clocks, and dahlias back to their homeland from South and Central America. Even so, the trickle of annuals was eclipsed by a veritable tide of exotic new perennials.

The real explosion of annuals would wait for the Industrial Revolution of the nineteenth century. In the meantime, the influence of women in gardening would set the stage for their arrival in gardens of the Old and New World alike.

THE QUEEN'S PASSION

When William and Mary ascended to the English throne in 1689—they are, incidentally, the only British monarchs to have been jointly proclaimed as King and Queen, he as the Dutch prince, William of Orange, and Mary as a princess of the house of Stuart—gardening fashion was in royal and talented hands. No English sovereigns before or since have taken such an active role in horticulture. William concentrated on refurbishing the gardens at Hampton Court to suit the new east front of the palace designed by Sir Christopher Wren. Queen Mary indulged her passion for exotic flowers and sent one of her gardeners to the colony of Virginia to collect specimens for her. She felt compelled to apologize for the money she spent on her hobby, which she admitted, "drew an expense after it." She noted, however, that it was her only extravagance, and since it "employed many hands, she hoped it would be forgiven her." She need not have worried about the judgment of history. Any true gardener, who can justify almost any plant purchase as absolutely essential, would not hold Queen Mary accountable and would, most likely, view her as a role model.

Daniel Defoe, of *Robinson Crusoe* fame, noted the influence of William and Mary, stating that, "in a few years fine gardens and fine houses began to grow up in every corner" of the land, and "the alteration is indeed wonderful through the whole kingdom." William was preoccupied by a formal style of gardening, which was prevalent on the continent, using clipped hedges, topiary, and elaborate geometric beds. It was imitated across the country, and in the American colonies. Yet it was Mary's love of flowers which was to outlive her husband's topiary. Queen Anne, who succeeded them, ordered all the manicured boxwood hedges removed, as she disliked their scent, but it portended ill for formality, which was swept away by the landscape movement of the eighteenth century. Anne's love of flowers is remembered in the name of Queen Anne's Lace, *Daucus carota*, a popular naturalized annual wildflower.

Princess Charlotte of Mecklenburg-Strelitz, who came to England in 1761 to marry George III, was a devoted student of botany. She was instructed, along with her daughters (she had fifteen children), in the fine art of botanic drawing. "There is not a plant in the gardens of Kew," wrote her botanist teacher Robert Thornton, "but has either been drawn by her gracious Majesty, or some of the Princesses, with a grace and skill. . . ." The Queen, who was the first royal patron of the Horticultural Society, is commemorated by the genus of exotic bird-of-paradise flowers, *Strelitzia*, not to mention four varieties of apples and, presumably, the dessert dish "Apple Charlotte."

The French court was in the throes of botanical passions as well, although royal women rarely drew. Pierre-Joseph Redouté was court painter during this turbulent period, and his patrons included, in order, Princess Adelaide, Queen Marie Antoinette, Empress Josephine, and finally, Marie-Amelie, wife of Louis Philippe. This royal patronage enabled Redouté to paint unprecedented and unequalled works. Color

Sixteenth-century missionaries in the New World sent the seeds of Nasturtium, *Tropaeolum majus*, OPPOSITE, to astonished European botanists. Pots of perennials and annuals, ABOVE, line a dooryard garden. Showy golden-orange *Gazania rigens*, BELOW, arrived in 1812 from southern Africa and was promptly dubbed Treasure Flower.

printing was almost prohibitively expensive, and each of his new books of lithographs incurred him more debt. Redouté was never a wealthy man, but he was famous. He was labelled then as the "Raphael of Flowers," and later, as the "Rembrandt of Roses," although today the name Redouté speaks for itself.

Empress Josephine's gardens at Chateau Malmaison were legendary, and all manner of exotic plants were found growing there. She was justifiably proud of her gardens, but she did not possess the generous na-

ture of most gardeners. She procured the very rare new dahlias from Spain, and her annual displays of them were the envy of every aristocratic lady. As the story goes, since Josephine would not part with so much as a single plant, a lady of the court worked her wiles on one of the gardeners, who secretly passed stolen tubers to her. When the foolish woman revealed her new dahlias the following summer, Josephine banished her from the court, sacked the gardener, and ordered that dahlias were never to be grown in her gardens again.

Daucus carota, Queen Anne's Lace, FAR LEFT, commemorates the Queen's love of flowers. Antique
Gomphrena globosa and modern 'Summer Madness' petunia combine effortlessly, LEFT. Empress Josephine came to loathe
dahlias—although not for their beauty—such as these, ABOVE, enhanced by an edging of *Senecio cineraria*.

BOTANY FOR LADIES

The royal example made botanical study and drawing sought-after accomplishments. In *Flora Bedfordiensis* (1798), C. Abbott wrote "that the fair daughters of Albion have evinced a zeal and ardour in botanical researches which has not only done the highest honour to themselves, but have eminently contributed to rescue these pursuits from unmerited reproach, and to impart to them, if not superior value, at least a superior currency of fashion." The study of botany had become easier to pursue, for either sex, after Linnaeus simplified matters by grouping similar plants (based on methods of reproduction) into families and genus. Under his system, which was widely adopted shortly after he presented it in *Species Plantarum* in 1753, each species was entitled to one adjective to describe it and to distinguish it from the other members of its genus and family. Appended to the genus name, this descriptive species name is known as the specific epithet or the binomial. For example, the spherical heads of an annual species of *Iberis*, commonly called Globe Candytuft, deemed that it should be known as *Iberis umbellata*; the second word refers to the arrangement of the flowers in umbels.

Linnaeus' classifications were based on the study of plant methods of reproduction. That the system was sexual was discreetly kept from the ladies. Lord Bute's *Botanical Tables* (1785), which he states is "composed solely for the Amusement of the Fair Sex," also carries the disclaimer that "no improper terms will be found in it." Counting the number of styles and stamens of each flower, without the slightest notion of their purpose, brought botany within the realm of any young lady who could count to twelve.

Botanical books written especially for women were in great demand. Among them were *Ladies' Botany* (1834) by John Lindley, not to be confused with *Botany for Ladies* (1842) by Jane Loudon, and Maria Jackson's extremely circumspect *Botanical Dialogues for the Use of Schools* (1797). Mrs. Loudon was the most important of the three, and certainly she influenced gardeners strongly during the first half of her century. With her husband John Claudius Loudon—who ranks highly among gifted horticulturists—she cultivated an extraordinary London garden. They grew nearly every plant known at the time, and the influence of their relatively small garden (tended by Mrs. Loudon in her wide-brimmed hat and long dress, for her husband had suffered the amputation of an arm) was felt far and wide. The Loudons were to horticulture what the Barrett-Brownings were to literature. Years after Mrs. Loudon's death in 1858, Maria Theresa Earle recognized the value of her books. She instructed that the volumes "are often to be picked up, very cheap, at secondhand shops, and I strongly recommend all ladies interested in gardening to buy them whenever they can lay their hands on them."

The list of women influential in horticulture should also include Elizabeth Kent, who was enormously successful at growing and writing about the plants she grew in pots on the roof of her house in St. Paul's Churchyard in London, and

The charming flowers of Globe Candytuft, BELOW, found an enduring home in cottage gardens upon arrival from Crete in 1739; they came to be known by the folk name Billy-Come-Home-Soon.

Louisa Johnson, who wrote *Every Lady Her Own Flower Gardener* in 1840. A review of the day stated unconditionally that "All lady floriculturists should possess it," which most of them certainly did, since the book went through fourteen editions before 1859.

Daughters of seed-house merchants often contributed to the family firm by illustrating plants for catalogues. William Curtis's *Botanical Magazine*, founded in 1787 (now titled *The Kew Magazine*) engaged the talents of many women botanical illustrators almost from its inception.

WOMEN IN AMERICA

The first notable woman botanist in America was Jane Colden, the daughter of a lieutenant governor in colonial New York. Encouraged by her father, a naturalist and correspondent of Linnaeus, she became a pioneer in the field of botany. She explored the wilds along the Hudson River in New York and by 1758 had written an illustrated account detailing four hundred species of native flora. It was never published, but after her death in 1766 it was sent to Sir Joseph Banks at Kew Gardens and is now in the British Museum.

During the nineteenth century, young American ladies pursued botanical studies with the same fervor as their European counterparts. Dr. Baldwin of Wilmington, Delaware, reported in 1811 that "a love for Botanical Science is fast progressing in our happy country." He found himself engaged in giving lectures "principally to young ladies, who are enamoured of the science." He tells of a young suitor who inquired of a pretty belle about the flowers in the bouquet she held. She proceeded to rattle off the common names, followed by the Latin genus and species. "The beau was so humiliated and confounded, that he betook himself to the science, the better to qualify him for her company." It's a pity young women don't study flowers and carry nosegays today—with such an effective brush-off at their disposal.

THE VICTORIAN ERA

Women became increasingly involved in practical horticulture. "It is a very nice study for ladies, and one which in England engages the attention of everyone, from Queen Victoria down, to arrange in winter the beds, and the flowers to fill them, for the summer decorations of the garden . . . ," remarked Thomas Meehan in 1872. He further stated that, "This practice has been gradually growing in England for the past 30 years, until now it is the universal winter employment of all ladies of taste. . . ." A fashionable flower garden of the latest annuals became an important feature of the well-run household, and played an important role in society. It was associated with love, beauty, and nature—three things the Victorians esteemed and idealized. Women were supposed to have a "natural" affinity for flowers and an "instinctive" love of gardens, where they were often symbolically confined. Many Victorians held that nature had given both flowers and women beauty and fragility, and to some they were practically one and the same. Consider Tennyson's poem "Maud," a passage of which reads:

> Rosy is the West,
> Rosy is the South,
> Rosy are her cheeks,
> And a rose in her mouth.

One almost feels compelled to break into a chorus of "Sugar in the morning, Sugar in the evening . . ." Yet despite her frail condition, the lady of the house often ran the household and garden with an iron hand. While she was involved in only the least rigorous chores, like gathering and arranging bouquets—such things as her feeble body could endure—the woman was the superintendent of the garden. If the family could afford a hired staff, she had to supervise their work; if not, she supervised her spouse.

To understand the Victorian garden is to understand the Victorian mind. To nurture a garden was a sign of a happy and harmonious family. The promise of love, often offered in an enchanted garden setting, was fulfilled and demonstrated in a garden built by a happy marriage. "A Picture," by poet Dora Greenwell paints a familiar Victorian scene:

From the wild Marigold, *Tagetes erecta*, BELOW, sprang a race of hybrids. Bells of Ireland, RIGHT, is native to the eastern Mediterranean region. FAR RIGHT, colonial American women valued *Xeranthemum annuum* for drying.

> It was in autumn that I met
> Her whom I love; the sunflowers bold
> Stood up like guards around her set,
> And all the air with mignonette
> Was warm within the garden old;
> Beside her feet the marigold
> Glowed star-like, and the sweet-pea sent
> A sigh to follow as she went
> Slowly adown the terrace;—there
> I saw thee, oh my love! and thou wert fair.

The poem goes on, of course, and suffice it to say that no one has ever been fairer or more beloved. The garden of annuals described sounds lovely—fresh and sweet. By contrast, the unhappy Miss Havisham's decrepit house, in Charles Dickens's *Great Expectations*, is surrounded by decay. The metaphor was clear—the pitiful old maid had never realized her dream of marriage, and her gardens fell to ruin.

Women, at least in gardening choices, began to exert their muscle. Fancy new-fangled contraptions such as lawnmowers were the province of men, but the women increasingly controlled the content of their gardens. The seed companies began to slant their advertising to appeal to feminine tastes. The flowers for cutting, many annuals among them, were in great demand. By the beginning of this century, much of popular garden literature was directed toward women.

We must not forget that in the past, especially during this era, horticultural books were written not from one gardener to another, but by garden owners for other garden owners. We find such labor-intensive advice in a late nineteenth-century garden manual, "If your peach tree grows too vigorously, have *your man* [italics mine] cut each leaf in half." I do not know if this would sap the tree's vigor; it would certainly sap mine.

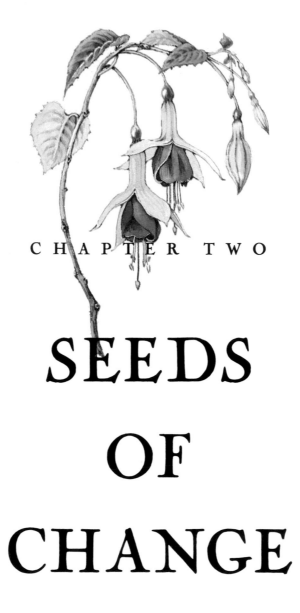

CHAPTER TWO

SEEDS

OF

CHANGE

HE KNOWS HIS RED SWEET WILLIAMS,
AND THE STOCKS THAT COST HIM DEAR,
THAT WELL SET ROW OF CRIMSON STOCKS,
FOR HE BOUGHT THE SEED LAST YEAR.

Mary Howitt, "Poor Man's Garden," circa 1870.

THE DAYS AFTER CHRISTMAS, for gardeners, mean immersing themselves in the seed catalogues for the unveiling of the latest annual introductions. This universal gardening experience has been repeated since the firm of Robert Furber in Kensington, considered England's most fashionable nursery at the time, sent out the first book-form catalogue about 1725.

The early catalogues also provide us with a look into the selections and practices of the day. By the beginning of Queen Victoria's reign in 1837, some annuals had deep historical roots in England and America. Balsams, cockscombs, nasturtiums, mignonettes, hollyhocks, and marigolds were already considered old-fashioned.

The face of horticulture was changed by the Industrial Revolution, as the impact of new technology transformed society. Progress was terribly important to the serious Victorian mind, which appears to have been intensely preoccupied with order and propriety. English and American Victorians were often of a single mind, and never have cultural ties been as close. The Industrial Revolution created the new urban society in both countries which was dominated by decidedly cosmopolitan ideas. The "cult of domesticity" deemed the home a secure haven of order and a stronghold of morality in an ever-changing world, not unlike our obsession about "the family" today. During the Victorian era, writers literally preached the necessity of growing flowers. In *Gardener's Monthly* of 1872, Thomas Meehan instructed that, "Flowers stimulate industry as well as lighten toil. For we must have them. We are cold without them, but to have them requires study, patient culture, and untiring determination." Whether Meehan enjoyed his garden seems secondary; growing flowers was a moral obligation.

The standard of living rose dramatically during this period. The result was a literate middle class with money to spend on gardens. Cheaper paper manufactured from wood pulp and steam-driven printing presses made it possible for seed houses to target large audiences on a national scale. New American railroads and highways, as well as low postal rates, provided cheap and quick access to mail-order consumers.

A copper boiler, LEFT, is planted with *Southern Star, Oxypetalum caeruleum,* originally named *Tweedia* after J. Tweedie.

THE SEED MERCHANTS

David Landreth started the first American seed company in 1784 in Philadelphia. The city became the center of the American seed business, and by the end of the next century more than a dozen firms were located there, the most famous being W. Atlee Burpee. Other major cities of the Northeast boasted important seed businesses. Joseph Breck founded his firm in Boston in 1818, and Peter Henderson started his company in Jersey City in 1847. Both men were prolific and influential writers. Gardeners had been dependent on European firms for annual seeds, and the new companies waged an aggressive campaign to capture the home market. The Landreth firm championed its "American Pedigree Seeds." Its 1886 catalogue advised, "Foreign seeds at best never have . . . the same vitality and vigor of growth as the hard, dry, ripened American seed, and when the soft, immature crops of Europe are subjected to the damp of an ocean passage, their already diminished vitality falls quite 12–15% additional."

Patriotism and propaganda weren't always enough to sell seeds to gardeners who had developed a taste for the exotic, and competition was strong with European merchants until the 1870s, when higher duties on imported goods gave American growers a decided home advantage. The

annual wildflowers of the Western American states had a considerable impact on the public during the second half of the nineteenth century; growers on either side of the Atlantic scrambled to provide seeds of the new exotics to an enamoured market. These new flowers symbolized discovery and progress, and clarkia, collinsia, Drummond's Phlox, gaillardia, California Poppy, and gilia became status symbols. The seedsmen extolled the virtues of the new introductions, and sought to breed hybrids with new colors and forms. Many British writers suffered from the misimpression that all American soil was acidic, and recommended their readers add peat and sand to accommodate these new plants. Success was, understandably, elusive.

Released from the confines of carpet bedding, Dusty Miller, RIGHT, shines with *Sedum spectabile* in a naturalistic garden.

Despite the lack of color pictures in the first seed catalogues—gorgeous lithographs became a feature later—present-day gardeners would feel nearly at home reading them. What may be somewhat bewildering is the inclination by some nurserymen to name hybrids as separate species, complete with Latin names. (Under the accepted rules of botany today, only "unaltered" plants deserve classification as separate species.) Variations created or selected by human hands—hybrids of two or more species or cultivated varieties, "cultivars," selected by sharp-eyed plantsmen—are now called by English names. The first (and now extinct) *Petunia* hybrids—of which there were soon to be legions—exemplify the old style of using Latinized names. Among these early hybrids were *maxima alba* (large white), *rosea grandiflora* (large bright rose), *fimbriata flore pleno* (double fringed), and *venosa grandiflora* (large, veined flowers). There was little standardization in naming, but it is surprising how most firms used scientific names, however carelessly spelled. Gradually there was a shift from Latin to common, or "fancy," names, as seedsmen became sophisticated in advertising. 'Black-throated Superbissima' was a W. Atlee Burpee Company hybrid developed after the Civil War; its name was descriptive and alluring,

as well as having a Latin ring of authority to it. As the century closed, names like 'Snowball' and 'Brilliant Rose' proliferated in the catalogues.

Seedsmen further discovered that names such as 'Victoria' Aster, 'Glasgow Prize' Cockscomb, and 'Crystal Palace Gem' Nasturtium, which reflected important people, places, and events of the times, improved sales. So it became common practice to introduce new annual novelties each year with catchy fancy names, although sometimes the only "new and improved" feature of a new hybrid was its name. Shirley Hibberd was disgusted by this misrepresentation, and told the readers of *The Amateur's Flower Garden* "the only way to insure seed worth growing is to go to a house *known* to be trustworthy, and pay a good price for it." Apparently even in 1871, gardeners got what they paid for.

So successful were the seed merchants that their influence was felt around the world. When plant hunter Frank Kingdon-Ward visited remote, previously unexplored regions of Tibet, he was amazed to find in one village a riotous courtyard garden of hollyhocks, sunflowers, pansies, stocks, geraniums, and nasturtiums—flowers of English and American gardens. The local governor had secured tins of Sutton's seeds from Calcutta.

BEDDING OUT

Tastes have changed—more than once—and so have our gardens. During the "high" Victorian era, the large estates, clipped and manicured by a legion of gardeners, and carpeted by thousands of annual bedding plants, set the trends. Ironically, it was a romantic notion about the formal gardens of the seventeenth century that inspired this drastic new look. Gardens of Georgian England had been rather restrained, and it had always heretofore been thought a major mistake to plant two flowers of the same kind next to

one another. Grouping identical plants in one bed was a progressive, if not downright radical, idea that was immediately embraced. Sir Joseph Paxton, gardener for the Duke of Devonshire, wrote in 1836, "Grouping, or arranging showy plants, en masse, has of late years become so general in all good gardens. . . ." He went on to advance the new schemes, stating, ". . . There are some who advocate beds with mixed plants . . . still they never have that striking effect that the same beds would have if filled with suitable plants, arranged in groups, and in large flower gardens we

Rows of *Ageratum houstonianum* and Coleus, RIGHT, bear the stamp of Victorians. Hot color floods a bed of marigolds and Four o'clocks, *Mirabilis jalapa*, OPPOSITE.

think them decidedly bad." Victorians were amused, decidedly, and by mid-century had lost their heads.

Theories were discussed about the new science of optics, and color theorist Robert Hendrie instructed in 1842 that, "A pleasing arrangement of colour is necessary in order to gratify the eye, and for this purpose a simultaneous presentation of the three primitive colours RED, YELLOW, and BLUE . . . is required. . . ." The discussion goes on at length, but most gardeners never seemed to get beyond the first paragraph, and before long the flower garden looked like Bagdad in flames.

The vogue for bedding plants in America was led by the wealthy new magnates. They often fancied themselves as princes and built mansions, surrounded by suitable grounds in what they imagined to be the Italianate style. Gardens required huge sums of money and vast efforts and relied on the new tender annuals flowing into England from plant-hunters in the tropics. The new flowers could not be seeded in the open cool ground; they needed to be started early in greenhouses in order to develop and bloom during the summer.

The greenhouse was essential to the large-scale production of annuals. It was a by-product of the technological advances of the day—notably construction with cast-iron supports and the availability of larger, less costly panes of glass (the enormous glass tax had been lifted). The Crystal Palace, built in 1851 for the Great Exhibition from Paxton's design, was only indirectly related to horticulture. Nevertheless, it fuelled the romantic imagination of gardeners. (The building was damaged by fire in 1936, and, sadly, de-

molished in 1941 because it served only too well as a landmark for enemy bombers.) Some horticulturalists, like Loudon, became deeply absorbed in possibilities of the glass house. He dreamed that a "a roof might be raised to the height of a hundred and fifty feet from the ground, to admit of the tallest oriental trees and the undis-

turbed flight of appropriate birds among their branches." He envisioned troops of monkeys and pools of tropical fish among the flowers. With a true visionary's fervor, Loudon proposed to case entire Russian towns in glass heated by hot water pipes. H. G. Wells was not to write of other such fantastic ideas until 1895's *The Time*

Machine, and greenhouses had mere utilitarian uses instead. They were stuffed to capacity with short, bright annuals from the tropics of the world. A greenhouse was a coveted status symbol, and the burgeoning middle class built them like mad, and threw carpets of bedding annuals on their lawns to impress passers-by.

Wealthy landowners with horticultural aspirations grew thousands of tender annuals in their new greenhouses, and competed with one another in extravagant displays to decorate (some might say desecrate) their grounds. Success was measured not only in the staggering number of plants grown in the garden, but in the ex-

Beds under a gazebo, ABOVE, overflow with Globe Amaranth, Love-lies-bleeding, and Snow-on-the-Mountain.
The proliferation of seed houses changed town gardens, OPPOSITE, making annuals and perennials available.

pense of a project, and the number of hours required to manage it. As the wealthy endeavored to outdo each other, they also strived to eclipse all gardening feats of the past. David Stuart points out in *The Garden Triumphant* that many "felt their past reflected too poorly on their present status," although he muses that ". . . in a garden like Chatsworth, owned by someone as enormously rich and aristocratic as the Duke of Devonshire, no particular need was felt to recreate lost grandeur; the duke was perfectly content to create grandeur now." It was estimated about 1850 that a fairly respectable landowner, with fairly simple designs, would need 100,000 plants to fill his beds in a single season. A private estate in Yonkers, New York, employed nearly sixty gardeners to raise and tend hundreds of thousands of bedding plants. The flowers were continuously changed from spring until autumn in ever-changing patterns; some plants spent as little as two to four weeks in the beds before being discarded.

The beds were often meant to be viewed from above, such as from a terrace or upper floor of a house, the better to appreciate the elaborate floral patterns. These designs often drew their inspiration from the complex knot gardens and parterres of Elizabethan and Tudor days. Innovations included straight or curving "ribbons" of color, and coats-of-arms and heraldic symbols were back in floral fashion. The nouveau-riche, who usually preferred not to proclaim their ancestry, consoled themselves with other innovations, like butterflies, clocks, or their names emblazoned across beds. (Every city park which proclaims the town's name in marigolds and

salvias can trace the custom back to this time. The annual Rose Bowl Parade, one suspects, would have put Victorians in a positive swoon.)

The intricate patterns of Oriental and Caucasian carpets, so popular in homes, were replicated outdoors with flowers.

These were the true "carpet beds," and were probably the greatest achievement of this vogue. Foliage plants, such as coleus, alternanthera, iresine, and even beets, were important components, as well as blooming plants like geraniums that were prevented from flowering, which would have spoiled the pattern made by the leaves. These fancy-leaved geraniums, with bands of colors in green, gold, cream, and red, were bred strictly for their foliage patterns. One old hybrid that still survives to this day, 'Madame Salleroi', was perfect for this use, in that the haughty lady has never even attempted to bloom. The color schemes (never a Victorian strong point) of the carpet beds were remarkably restrained. All shades of green, silver, bur-

gundy, russet, yellow, and glaucous blue foliage imitated the subdued tones of the rugs. One bed planted in 1871 in Woolwich, England, contained almost three thousand plants and measured twelve by thirty-four feet. It was highly praised at the time. A farsighted writer and gardener, known to us now only as Miss Hope, suggested using unusual perennials for carpet beds, like sedums, houseleeks, euonymus, and heuchera. The ideas she espoused in *Gardens and Woodlands* (1881) set the framework for the transition to the "ground cover bedding" of today.

Miss Hope was ahead of her day, and annuals ruled it. The general standards reflected a desire for uniform dwarf annual plants that, if they were required to do so, would bloom early, long, and brightly. Every attempt was made to force conformity; free-growing plants like clematis and *Salvia patens* were mercilessly pegged down and pruned into unnatural postures. Those annuals (and perennials) that would not fit such a mold were never part of the bedding plant schemes and were grown, if at all, only in cutting gardens or unfashionable cottage gardens. "It is much the rage," wrote a disgruntled George Glenny in 1848, "to obtain new plants and neglect old ones. . . ." (The modern gardener finds that many hybrids offered today are suitable only for re-creations of Victorian gardens, and that their stiff habit is inappropriate for other designs. In that case, unimproved species are often more adaptable.)

A few larger and more dramatic annuals, such as amaranthus and the Castor-oil Plant, were often featured as "dot" or accent plants—dead center in geometric beds—or as lawn specimens. These subtropical effects were enormously appealing to some.

The decline of the bedding craze resulted largely from the incredible cost in labor, but it also reflected a growing disenchantment for rigidly geometric gardens. Summing up this attitude towards viewing vast blocks of identical flowers, Henry Mitchell concludes in *The Essential Earthman* that, ". . . often the main pleasure people get from them is discovering one yellow tulip in a bed of five hundred red ones." He goes on to consider the motivation for planting flowers in such blocks, saying that, "Those who perpetuate it are probably dull sorts who worry a great deal about colors clashing, and doing the wrong thing. The wholesome, ebullient gardener need not emulate it." It is interesting to speculate whether economic considerations propelled the artistic revolution against carpet bedding, although the new aesthetic direction must have come as a great relief to many a manor owner burdened by keeping up with some semblance of fashion. As the era of grand bedding schemes waned, the writings and examples of William Robinson and Gertrude Jekyll, who advocated the informal perennial border, revolutionized the flower garden in England and America. Miss Jekyll wrote stingingly about the lack of artistry, saying, "In the days of less enlightened gardening, . . . anything that was aimed at in the way of colouring was nearly always some violent contrast, or the putting together of crudely coloured flowers; a pleasant harmony was scarcely thought of. Now that more thoughtful ways prevail we try for something better than garishness—we try for

the nobler colour-quality of sumptuous splendour. In acquiring this . . . the eye and mind are filled with a consciousness of delightful satisfaction of attainment instead of their being, as it were, rudely attacked, and, in the case of the more sensitive among us, actually shocked by a harsh crudity that has some of the displeasing qualities of vulgarity."

The Industrial Revolution, which had made the new wealth that fuelled the fires of Victorian style, eventually crushed it. Gone are the ostentatious displays. The "bothy" boys of England (named for the common quarters they shared), who served as indentured apprentices to the head gardeners, no longer care for the greenhouses and display beds of the manor houses. Only the remnants of these gar-

Bedding schemes, ABOVE, often incorporate cannas for a subtropical effect.
A sylvan setting, OPPOSITE, showcases *Lantana camara*, sage, and petunias.

dens remain, and the flowers have been abandoned. Some flowers in old catalogues are still to be found in modern ones, but many have vanished, indicating the plant may be gone as well. As the fledgling science of hybridization advanced, new varieties were created almost overnight, while old strains and hybrids disappeared as quickly. There are very few hybrids of the last century still available. Unlike perennial hybrids, some of which survived cossetted in old gardens, annuals vanished quickly. Even those that seed themselves "revert" to the characteristics of their parent species. Very few of the old violas are known to exist, and still fewer pansies. Most of the hollyhocks, asters, and calceolarias— sometimes called pocket-book flowers— are gone, victims of disease. Trouble was already brewing in the last quarter of the nineteenth century, when Hibberd complained, "It is not uncommon for all the calceolarias in the country to perish about the middle of July, leaving the parterres they should have adorned with masses of golden flowers abominably ugly with their withered stumps, or, at the best, obnoxious blanks." Double verbenas, wallflowers, and snapdragons appear to be extinct, and only a handful of hybrids of other annual species are known.

Even flowers such as fuchsia, coleus, and geranium—plants easily propagated by cuttings—are represented by few hybrids from Victorian days. The continuity in a family or nursery business that might ensure an old hybrid's survival for a hundred years or more is exceedingly rare. On the other hand, most of the unimproved species, which vary little from generation to generation, have survived.

CHAPTER THREE

THE MYSTIQUE

OF

ANNUALS

ONE FOR THE ROOK,
ONE FOR THE CROW,
ONE TO DIE,
AND ONE TO GROW.

SO GOES AN OLD PROVERB about sowing annuals thickly. Planting a seed and watching it grow is as old as agriculture. Mankind has an incredible fascination with the process, and derives great satisfaction from the results. Seeds of annuals are grown throughout the world, and every culture has evolved rituals, customs, and superstitions about their planting and cultivation. Primitive man, who had only the slightest inkling of the scientific facts that determine the mechanics of germination and plant growth, had to rely on trial and error. Early gardeners found that certain practices ensured success, but not always for the reason they may have thought. Some old wives' wisdom in the garden has been found to have merit, and other has been discounted. Today's gardener has the advantage of the cumulative knowledge of botanists and horticulturists at his or her disposal, yet it is amazing how the lore of superstition and ritual still governs our garden practices.

The lunar debate, for example, has been going on for some time. Is it advisable to sow seed or transplant only with a waxing, never a waning, moon? It was thought the rhythms of the moon affected plant growth, and that it was more likely to rain immediately after a new moon, which, of course, would be ideal. Many gardeners still determine planting dates by the moon; some of us, who haven't the slightest clue whether the moon is on the wax or wane, muddle through somehow.

Farmers in Lincolnshire are reported to have once dropped their trousers each spring and sat in the soil of their fields. If they felt comfortable, they commenced planting—fully clothed, we assume. If the farmers became cold and damp, the spring planting was postponed. Their discomfort signalled that the seeds would fare poorly, as they would rot in the cold earth. Old herbals recommended not only consulting lunar signs, but to sow seed while naked. If the weather was warm enough to allow the gardener to go without clothes, it would be warm enough for seeds to germinate. It was thought God would look more favorably on the humble gardener, even if his neighbors did not.

Some flowers were helpful in predicting the weather. Calendulas and clover, it was held, would contract their leaves at the approach of a storm. The Scarlet Pimpernel, *Anagallis arvensis*, was used similarly as a barometer, and came to be known as the Poor Man's Weatherglass. If the flowers opened wide in the morning, there would be fair weather, but if the petals remained closed, rain was imminent.

The simple country people in England and America, who grew plants for food and pleasure in bountiful but humble gardens, were responsible for the revival of interest in antique annuals. Those gardeners had neither the means nor the inclination to follow the dictates of the fashion-conscious manors, and so evolved a style of gardening based only on the rules of good plantsmanship. It is ironic that the gardens of the "cottagers" exert perhaps the greatest influence on the fashion of today. Their unmannered and unpretentious style is carefully copied by designers, though the result is rarely as successful.

Skeptics point out that the cottage garden has been idealized, and that in some

Pot Marigold, *Calendula officinalis*, and China Aster, *Callistephus chinensis*, OPPOSITE, flank a drive. The influence of cottage gardens shows, ABOVE, in a grouping of Tickseed, Jasmine Tobacco, Morning Glory, and Indian Blanket.

ways, it was yet another fantasy of the Victorians. As society in the nineteenth century rapidly changed from an agrarian to an industrialized one, there was a wave of nostalgia. The new urban majority looked at country life through the images of writers who portrayed rosy-cheeked cottagers living an idyllic existence. What may indeed be true is that the cottage gar-

deners were just as likely to grow the newest flowers, raised from a penny packet of seeds, as were the gardeners of grand estates. Lithographs of the period, in fact, show thatched cottages ringed with bedding displays. These were, thankfully, a minority.

Even to this day, rural gardens are often more truly representative of the idealized cottage garden. The seed catalogues may

have enlarged the diversity of the cottage garden, but it has never disappeared. Margery Fish marvelled at "the uncanny way the cottagers had of finding and keeping a good plant." This "champion of weeds," as she was known for her efforts to preserve the old-fashioned flowers, tells of wallflowers and snapdragons growing in old walls, and how "Pansies and Forget-me-Nots flower under the currant bushes, nasturtiums frolic among the carrots, and old apple trees give welcome shade."

In cottage and farmhouse gardens, annuals, vegetables, shrubs, vines, bulbs, and perennials were planted in seemingly effortless harmony. Cuttings and seeds were traded between gardeners, and favorites were grown by generation after generation. Flowers were tended and picked throughout the summer, and seeds were saved each autumn. Flowers were a part of village and rural life. They were given for joyous occasions, like births and anniversaries. They decorated the village church on

saints' days and for weddings and funerals.

Flowers held many associations for those who grew them. Young girls have used various methods to determine their future husbands, and one is struck by their dogged determination, if not downright obsession. We all know the common refrain, "He loves me, he loves me not," repeated while plucking daisy petals. In parts of England, a maiden would pick a handful of Bachelor's Buttons in the morning—as many as she had prospective suitors—and give each blossom the name of a fellow. She would tuck them in her blouse, and at the end of the day, the flower which had fared the best held the name of her intended. (Mind you, since the flowers are nearly identical, there may have been a bit of cheating when the results were examined.) In another ritual, a maiden might pick a flower at night, reciting:

> New moon, true moon,
> Happy may I be,
> Whoever is my true love
> This night may I see.

After carefully tucking the flower in her left stocking, which was placed under her pillow, the lass hoped to see her groom in a dream. Once she knew his identity, she still needed to be sure of his love. She then might take the petal of a poppy and place it in her palm. If, when she smacked it smartly, it made a loud pop, her lover would be true. (These things take practice, and it is not clear just how many times a girl might be allowed to repeat the procedure until she achieved the desired result.)

OPPOSITE, Jasmine Tobacco softens a sea of yellow California poppies, marigolds, and *Coreopsis grandiflora*. Forget-me-nots, ABOVE, are shaded by *Gunnera manicata*.

USES FOR ANNUALS

Gardeners often feel the same affection for favorite annuals they knew and loved in childhood, perhaps because they were handed down through many generations. Annuals and biennials should not be considered just as garden fillers, although they are frequently used to fill gaps before perennials and shrubs have reached maturity. Those that regularly seed themselves each

ABOVE, *Cleome hassleriana* dots this sophisticated planting. Bachelor's Buttons, BELOW, once told maidens of their true love.

year, such as pansies, Forget-me-nots, Bachelor's Buttons, Jasmine Tobacco, and Sweet Alyssum, provide surprises by appearing in unexpected spots and can overcome self-conscious and overly-mannered designs. The key is to recognize the stray seedling as valuable, although rogueing out unwanted volunteers is equally important.

Shorter-growing plants make excellent edging for flower beds. Edging can be formal and straight, or more relaxed. We might all take a lesson in edging from a master, as when Gertrude Jekyll tells us in *Annuals and Biennials* how "to let the plants accompany good groups of taller things as a kind of free carpeting; the dwarf plant not only coming to the front, but running a little way back between the others, in such as ways as to be quite informal." Annuals of medium height can be treated similarly, deeper within a bed, to form interlocking patterns in a jig-saw style.

Vining annuals are commonly used to screen unsightly objects or decorate arbors and trellises, but they may also be grown at the back of beds. By training them forward, vines such as sweet peas and trailing nasturtiums can cover the yellowing foliage of perennial poppies. An old-fashioned custom is to grow climbers on "pea sticks" in a free-standing teepee.

Tall annuals are useful as dramatic accents at the back of beds, although they can bring a sense of intimacy to a small garden when tucked into a small space. The small doorway gardens of the American Southwest feature towering hollyhocks, and I recall tall sunflowers growing against the whitewashed walls of the first school I attended. Taller plants are planted effectively as quick-growing hedges

or screens. In the vegetable garden, these screens may delineate the boundaries between vegetable rows and a cutting garden. Many vegetable gardens these days are pretty as well as practical when flowers for cutting are interplanted with lettuce, turnips, and beans.

Cutting gardens have recently enjoyed a revival in interest. The garden of Celia Thaxter, which inspired many of the paintings of impressionist Childe Hassam, has recently been restored on the island of Appledore, off the coast of Maine. Its profusion of annual poppies, spider flowers, and

Pink Hawksbeard, *Crepis rubra*, ABOVE, is a pretty annual addition to borders or rockeries.

tickseeds—remember, this was a functional garden—is captured in lovely paintings that charm us as much as the public of the late 1800s.

Besides providing a continuous source of flowers for bouquets, annuals can be employed for other purposes. Hardy annuals that can be seeded directly in the ground during autumn or late winter can disguise the yellowing foliage of spring-

blooming bulbs. As they grow, the leaves of malva or nigella will quickly screen the unsightly leaves of tulips, daffodils, and the like; to ensure that enough energy is directed back into the bulbs for bloom the next year, their leaves must be allowed to remain until they wither. Annuals serve to unify plantings of changing perennials throughout the season. They may be incorporated into a traditional border, or in almost any style of garden.

Adventurous rock gardeners plant annuals to extend the display after the spring-blooming alpine plants have finished, although the selection of appropriate types is crucial. Rock gardeners have traditionally eschewed annuals. As Geoffrey Charlesworth writes in *The Opinionated Gardener*, "It is hard to buck the consensus when it includes just about every rock-garden writer who ever set pen on paper. There is either a snide dismissal of annuals or a conspiracy of silence. . . ." While he hastens to point out that "petunias look ridiculous next to saxifrages," plantsman Charlesworth recommends fifty or so annuals suitable for, and desirable in, a rock garden, among them *Collinsia grandiflora*, *Crepis rubra*, *Dimorphotheca aurantiaca*, *Emilia flammea*, *Gilia capitata*, *Lupinus texensis*, *Nemophila maculata* and *N. menziesii*, *Nigella damascena*, *Phacelia tanacetifolia*, and *P. campanularia*.

Many of the gardens today are small, especially in cities. As outdoor living areas contract, the need for flowers in containers to brighten patios, terraces, balconies, porches, and rooftops has increased. Annuals have played a traditional role in this respect. Tubs and terra-cotta pots are as traditional as strawberries and cream at

Wimbledon. In fact, anything that holds soil has, at one time or another, been used as a planter. I recall a vogue for planting in old tractor tires, their edges peeled back; that trend, happily, has passed. Container gardening has a few differences from planting in the ground, but the principles of garden artistry are just as applicable.

Gardeners rarely plant in the nude today, to my knowledge (or else I am simply not abreast of the times), but the lure and mystique of annual flowers endures. There is something comforting in the flowers we grow from seed each year, perhaps because we feel a tangible link with the past, as well as with other kindred souls. Flowers are fleeting, but the urge to grow them is universal and timeless.

An informal edging, ABOVE, features *Lobularia maritima* and *Lobelia erinus*. The only thing Irish about Bells of Ireland, BELOW, is the color, used with blue Cupid's Dart and orange *Zauschneria californica*.

CHAPTER FOUR

A PORTFOLIO OF ANTIQUE ANNUALS

THE SHREWD AND CAPABLE WOMEN OF THE COLONIES
WHO ENTERED SO FREELY AND SUCCESSFULLY INTO
BUSINESS VENTURES FOUND THE SELLING OF FLOWER
SEEDS A CONGENIAL OCCUPATION, AND OFTEN ADDED
IT TO THE PURSUIT OF OTHER CALLINGS. I THINK IT
MUST HAVE BEEN VERY PLEASANT TO BUY PACKAGES
OF FLOWER SEED AT THE SAME TIME AND PLACE
WHERE YOU BOUGHT YOUR BEST BONNET, AND HAVE
ALL SENT HOME IN A BANDBOX TOGETHER; EACH
WOULD PROVE A MEMORIAL OF THE OTHER; AND LONG
AFTER THE GLORY OF THE BONNET HAD DEPARTED,
AND THE BONNET ITSELF WAS ASHES, THE THRIVING
SWEET PEAS AND LARKSPUR WOULD RECALL ITS
BECOMING CHARMS. Alice Morse Earle, Old Time Gardens, 1901

 No one can be certain where the Hollyhock, *Alcea rosea*, first grew, or when it arrived in the gardens of the Western world, but its story parallels the history of gardens as we know them. It has long been believed that the plant is native to China, but it has never been found growing wild. It is probably a natural hybrid between *A. setosa* of Turkey and *A. pallida* of Eastern Europe and Crete that was swept in all directions along the currents of the trade routes. Returning crusaders likely brought seed to England, for the "holyhock" is mentioned in *Feate of Gardening* by John Gardiner, a poem copied in manuscript in 1440, although it was probably written even earlier. *Hoc* was the old Anglo-Saxon word for mallow, and the association with the Crusades may have given it the virtue of being holy. William Turner wrote of "our common hoyoke" in his *New Herbal* of 1551, and the plant was widely grown, even though no two writers appear to have agreed on the spelling. Some have suggested that the leaves were used at one time to treat the swollen hocks of horses, and so was known as

"Hockleaf," but this may be considered a farfetched explanation.

"Hollihocks," wrote John Parkinson in 1629, "both single and double, of many and sundry colours, yeeld out their flowers like Roses on their tall branches, like Trees, to sute you with flowers when almost you have no other, to grace out your garden." He may have referred to midsummer, which before the influx of later-blooming annuals and perennials resulting from plant-hunting expeditions centuries later, was known as "the Dull Period." In some gardens it still is. French Huguenots, fleeing to England from religious persecution, brought new strains of seed with them. This "Outlandish Rose"—the similarity of the flowers to roses is noted by the binomial designation *rosea*, meaning rose-colored—focused new attention on hollyhocks.

The Latin name is from *althaia*, cure, and herbalists added the dried and powdered roots to wine to kill worms in children, prevent miscarriages, and prevent blood clots. Nicholas Culpeper, whose astrologically-inspired advice was taken very seriously in his day, prescribed the root to treat "incontinence of urine, immoderate menses, bleeding wounds, spitting of blood, the bloody flux, and other fluxes of the belly." Gardeners, past and present, have held a slightly more romantic notion of hollyhocks.

Sir Thomas Hanmer wrote late in the seventeenth century that, "The plant is fittest for courts or spacious gardens, being soe great and stately." Oddly enough, it is the cottage garden and farmyard where the image of hollyhocks is most enduring, not the grand estates. The plant was so

Alcea rosea Malvaceae

HOLLYHOCK

popular during the nineteenth century that it rivalled the dahlia in the number of hybrids. Single and double varieties were grown, ranging from pale yellow to near-black, and some were striped.

Nearly all these hybrids were wiped out almost overnight when rust disease struck. Caused by a fungus that also selectively attacks wheat and other crops, the plague was first mentioned in England in 1873. Hollyhocks in America fell victim almost simultaneously. While rust does not necessarily kill plants outright, the orange-brown patches grow on the undersides of leaves, weakening the plants. Interest in growing hollyhocks plummeted.

New England–style Hollyhock dolls dance on a rock wall, OPPOSITE. *Alcea rosea*, BELOW, arrived with returning Crusaders.

An attempt was made in England during the last century to grow *Alcea rosea* as a commercial crop. Two hundred eighty acres were planted with the intention of using the fibers of the stalks like hemp or flax, which is not as unlikely as it sounds; the cotton plant, *Gossypium hirsutum*, is a relative. The venture was unsuccessful, but the fields must have been lovely.

Hollyhocks are short-lived perennials, but are most often grown as annuals or biennials. They require a sunny garden position and benefit from rich soil and regular watering. The stems, which may grow to as much as ten feet, are clad with three-inch blossoms throughout midsummer. Plants with single flowers are often favored for informal gardens, but the double varieties are just as appropriate in period gardens. Rust disease is still a problem. The Romans held festivals to implore the rust gods not to attack their food crops; this remains almost as effective as modern controls. Fungicides and vigilance, however, have allowed hollyhocks to return.

As a child, I remember helping my sister fashion dolls from the flowers; these elegant "ladies" wore skirts of fine silky petals. The dolls had a distinctly Jamaican look, for their heads were made from opening buds (attached with a toothpick), so that they appeared to be wearing matching turbans. As an adult, I never met a gardener who remembered, or would admit, making hollyhock dolls, and I began to imagine they were peculiar to my sister. Only recently, a friend in Connecticut told me that she, too, had played with them, but with one minor difference—the seed pods were used for the heads. East coast hollyhock dolls wore no turbans.

It is unclear when the first amaranth was grown in England, but John Gerard, who published his *Herball* in 1597, grew *Amaranthus caudatus* and called it Great Purple Flower-Gentle. The species most likely originated in South America and advanced north through trading; the Aztecs called it Inca Wheat, and it was eaten as a cereal and used in ceremonies. At one point it was recorded that eighteen of the empire's granaries were filled with the small seeds. Spanish missionaries may have sent seed back to Europe. As early as 1665 it was called Love-lies-bleeding, partly because the drooping maroon flower heads may have suggested a flow of blood, but also because the old Greek name *amarantos* may have been at some point copied as *amoranthus*. The English took the French *amor* to heart, and associated the flowers with love in a most melancholy way; it was also called Floramor. (The French, on the other hand, made no such mistake, but their name for *A. caudatus* was even more grisly—they called it Nun's Scourge, for to the Gallic mind it suggested the flagellation of penitents.) *A. hypochondriacus*—the intriguing name means "of somber aspect"—is a similar species, although the flowers are held upright as opposed to the binomial name of *A. caudatus*, which means "with a tail."

Amaranthus
Amaranthaceae

You call it, "love-lies-bleeding" so you may,
Though the red flower, not prostrate only droops,
As we have seen it here from day to day,
From month to month, life passing not away.
                              William Wordsworth

Amaranthus caudatus LOVE-LIES-BLEEDING

Amaranthus tricolor JOSEPH'S COAT

The flower swags of *A. caudatus*, OPPOSITE, appealed to gardeners and poets
alike. The flowers of *A. tricolor*, ABOVE, are insignificant; the foliage is not.

Recent reclassification of this genus has rendered the meaning of *Amaranthus* nearly obsolete. An amaranth was originally an everlasting flower—the name means never-waxing-old or unfading—but Globe Amaranth is now *Gomphrena*, and most of the Elizabethan Floramors are currently called *Celosia*. The plants remaining include some very ornamental ones, as well as some decidedly un-ornamental food crops, none of which can be considered as true everlastings. The flower heads of *A. caudatus* do last for a long time in the garden.

Joseph's Coat, *A. tricolor*, which came from the Far East late in the sixteenth century, was one of the first tropical plants to make an impact in British gardens. Elizabethans were thrilled by its multicolored foliage (plants are highly variable and the flowers are insignificant), and Gerard excitedly described how ". . . everie leafe resembleth in colour the most fair and beautifull feather of a Parat," although he admitted that, "It farre exceedeth my skill to describe the beautie and excellencie of this rare plant called *Floramor.* . . ." Methinks he was too humble. The dark leaves are suffused with red at the base of the five-foot plants, but are sometimes brilliant carmine red on top. The fluorescent neon colors startled gardeners, for they were incomparable—the discovery of electricity was centuries away. Seeing was believing, but "molten fire" was as close as they could come in terms of description.

A. tricolor proved difficult to grow. William Hanbury, a distinguished gardener, writer, and clergyman, warned about 1770 that "many a Gardener has been ambitious of excelling his brother in shewing them in the greatest perfection, but many a Gardener, after repeated trials, has failed in his attempts." The trick, as the Victorians would learn, was to start the tender plant early in the greenhouse; as might be expected, Joseph's Coat then became a spectacular dot plant in bedding schemes.

Love-lies-bleeding was popular in the

A restoration of a Victorian garden, OPPOSITE, relies on the spectacle of Love-lies-bleeding for impact. John Milton chose the "immortal amarant," ABOVE, to crown angels in *Paradise Lost*.

nineteenth century as well, and it was sometimes grown as a lawn specimen. The tasselled flowers became, in fact, too well associated with stiff Victorian styles, and fell from favor. It does take imagination and discretion for the modern gardener to situate any of the amaranths to advantage. Their height, usually four feet or more, is accompanied by bulk—these are heavy-looking plants. Joseph's Coat imparts a tropical feeling to a planting. Several plants could be placed as focal points within a broad sweep of airy cosmos. Against a backdrop of tall dark shrubs, such as junipers or Smoke Bush, *Cotinus coggygria*, the effect would be smashing, although it could never be characterized as subtle. Those who hold no particular affection for these plants might consider the words of Hermon Bourne, written in 1833 but still valid. He noticed how after a rain shower or in the early morning, "it then appears to stand sparkling in dew-drops, or raindrops, like a cluster of rubies or crimson coral, bedropt with thousand sparkling gems or diamonds bright."

Species of *Amaranthus* grow best in full sun and need supplemental watering during dry spells, but no more than most common plants of the flower garden. They are adaptable to most soils, and the leaf coloration of Joseph's Coat is even more brilliant when it is grown in poor soil, although the plants may not grow as tall. The flowers of Love-lies-bleeding are long-lasting and dramatic in (large) arrangements.

Borago officinalis is one of the oldest annual flowers of the garden. It is mentioned in old herbals as early as 1265. Possibly native to Britain, it most likely jumped the English Channel by one means or another at a very early date. From the time of the ancient Greeks it has been added to drinks. Borage is probably the plant Homer called *nepenthe*, the juice of which was added to wine to relieve sadness. Gerard wrote in 1597 that, "The leaves and floures of Borage put into wine make men and women glad and merry, driving away all sadnesse, dulness and melancholie." That this merriment may have owed more to the wine than the Borage is debatable. Gerard quoted the old Latin saying, "I, Borage, bring alwaies courage," and the Latin name was said to be derived from a corruption of the word *corago*, from *cor*, heart, and *ago*, I bring (unfortunately, it's more likely the name comes from *burra*, a hairy garment). Tudor and Stuart needlework was laced with Borage blossoms, and since embroiderers used fresh flowers as models, the plant must have been widely grown.

In *The Countrie Housewife's Garden* (1617), William Lawson (presumably writing for an audience of country housewives, not as one himself), extolled the virtues of "Burrage and Bugloss (*Anchusa capensis*)." He wrote, ". . . they are exceedingly good Pot herbs, good for bees, and most comfortable to the heart and stomach." The leaves were sometimes eaten for their cucumber-like flavor, but it was the flowers that earned for the plant the folk name Cooltankard. Long before the invention of the

Borago officinalis Boraginaceae

BORAGE

Borage blossoms, ABOVE, float in claret cups. Stems of *B. officinalis*, OPPOSITE, bristle with fine hairs.

ice-cube, the flowers were found to bring a cooling taste to drinks. This phenomenon is due to the presence of nitre, often found in the flowers of the Boraginaceae. A claret cup—wine blended with lemon juice, brandy, sugar, fruit, and on occasion, the kitchen sink—has traditionally been garnished with Borage flowers. The flowers have long been candied like violets.

Borage cordials were at one time advised for treating heart conditions and consumption. A decoction of Borage and Yellow Fumitory, *Corydalis lutea*, was pre-scribed to cleanse the blood and treat ringworm. In a curious mix of medicine and poetry, Robert Burton wrote in *The Anatomy of Melancholy* (1621):

Borage and Hellebore fill two scenes,
Sovereign plants to purge the veins
Of melancholy, and cheer the heart
Of those black fumes which make it smart.

Since all species of *Helleborus* are highly poisonous, this cure could be less cheerful than hoped and, in fact, quite permanent.

Borage has been shuffled between herb and ornamental gardens for centuries. We draw no such distinction today—herb gardens are highly ornamental—and Borage is a charming, if unassuming, addition to any planting. The leaves and stems of the two-foot plants are clad with bristly hairs, giving them a silver cast. Close inspection of the flowers reveals five pointed petals of periwinkle blue arranged like a star. A dark cone of anthers protrudes from each pendulous blossom. This is not a flower for those who go for floral fireworks and whose gardens must be viewed from hovering aircraft to be truly appreciated.

Borage is easily raised from seed, either sown in open ground in early spring, or from windowsill-grown transplants. It flowers throughout the season, and is still "exceedingly good for bees." Once planted, it will often "volunteer" in succeeding years. An all-blue border would profit from its inclusion, and Borage is pretty with plants of silver foliage like *Santolina chamaecyparissus* and *Artemisia frigida*. It is a subtle companion for pale pink flowers, such as stock or Shirley Poppies. On a summer evening, the gardener might think Borage looks best floating in a glass of wine.

Gardeners have always called these annuals asters, a name they share with many perennial species. No one had the slightest difficulty in distinguishing them, but through the perversity of botany, they are now called *Callistephus*. The name is from *kallistos*, most beautiful, and *stephos*, a crown, which is all well and good, except it is so vapid as to be totally forgettable. The flowers, however, are not. When first grown in Paris in 1728—from seed sent from China—they created a sensation. The single white and red varieties were grown first, and the purple a few years later. Sir Horace Walpole was astonished during a visit in 1770 that "in the garden of Marshall de Biron at Paris, consisting of fourteen acres, every walk is buttoned on each side by lines of flower-pots, which succeed in their seasons. When I saw it, there were nine thousand pots of Asters. . . ." A fine sight surely, and it is notable that it precedes the epoch of Victorian extravagance.

China Asters became wildly popular in America. Hermon Bourne wrote in 1833 in *The Florist's Manual* how they were also called Fair Ladies' Stars, and, in capital letters, "THE EMBLEM OF RURAL HAPPINESS AND PIOUS ENJOYMENT." Seedsmen offered exotic new (but pious) variations each year—doubled, tripled, with blossoms mimicking dahlias, peonies, and ranunculus. *The Gardener's Chronicle* of December, 1887, describes the new Comet strain as resembling ". . . very closely that of a large-flowered Japanese Chrysanthemum. The petals are long and

Callistephus chinensis Compositae

CHINA ASTER

somewhat twisted or wavy or curled. . . ." Asters were easily manipulated by hybridists, and there was an urge among them to make them look like something else. They left the floral kingdom altogether in breeding the "Hedge-Hog" type, which had long quilled petals that were sharply pointed. One catalogue from 1867 describes them as "very curious." Indeed.

Top-notch hybrids from Germany were highly touted, despite the fact that people there called them "death-flowers." The association supposedly stemmed from a story about Elizabeth, Empress of Austria, who found her room in a Swiss hotel decorated with China Asters. She told her attendant the flowers gave her a feeling of foreboding, which proved correct, in that she was found the next day murdered by an Italian anarchist. (The assassination, incidentally, of her great-nephew Francis Ferdinand sparked the first World War.) It is also interesting to note that asters are forbidden from felicitous occasions in Japan, possibly due to their Chinese origin rather than out of respect for an Austrian empress.

It is difficult to associate China Asters with anything melancholy. Their color range, which still embraces various shades of the original white, red, and purple French seedlings, makes them favorites for cheerful bouquets. Do not believe a seed catalogue that promises a blue flower—the euphemism for purple is rampant. Single blooms, with the prominent daisy-like center, are sometimes preferred, but the double varieties are pretty, too. Despite intensive breeding in the nineteenth century, China Asters still possess a unique look that is distinctly old-fashioned (especially the two- to three-foot varieties for cutting; the dwarf ones are squat and rather undignified). A single plant may appear a bit stiff and awkward, but a thick patch of them is breathtaking.

The hybrids of the past fell victim to a disease known as "aster yellows," which stunts their growth, deforms the flowers, and is characterized by yellowing of the leaves. There is no cure for the disease, and infected plants should be removed promptly. To prevent the disease or its return, experienced gardeners commonly grow the plants in different locations each

Single forms of China Aster bloom amidst Pot Marigold,
Calendula officinalis, LEFT, and closely resemble the original wild species as it was
when discovered in China during the early eighteenth century.

year to thwart the soil-borne bacteria which is spread by leafhoppers.

Unlike most other annuals, asters do not benefit from dead-heading. In fact, they stop blooming. Individual plants only bloom for about a month, so it is best to extend their season by planting varieties that mature at different intervals, or sowing seeds at two-week intervals in the spring. Asters are shallow-rooted, so they benefit from a mulch to retain water in the soil. They grow best in a sunny location in fertile soil. If one is of royal birth, beware of premonitions of death.

Providing spectacular effects in flower beds and arrangements, China Aster, *Callistephus chinensis*, LEFT, was among the most popular flowers in days past. Hybridists manipulated the flower form of *C. chinensis* into novel shapes, including the long-stemmed quilled varieties, ABOVE.

Cleome hassleriana
Capparaceae

SPIDER FLOWER

These exotic flowers are native to South and Central America, and similar species are found in the southwestern United States. They are naturalized in many tropical countries, especially in Africa, and are sometimes found as garden escapees in southern states. *Cleome hassleriana* was first grown about 1810, and became a feature of dooryard gardens and grand estates.

Cleome is from the Greek *kleio*, meaning to shut, perhaps in reference to the petals—slender below and with wider upper halves—that curl by day during hot weather, and only extend themselves at sundown. The name was used by Theophrastus about 250 B.C. for some flower, but it is impossible that he had seen any plants from the as-yet-unknown New World. *C. hassleriana* was formerly classified as *C. speciosa* or misidentified as *C. spinosa* or *C. gigantea*, names under which it is usually found in seed catalogues.

The floral configuration of *Cleome hassleriana* is unusual. The flower clusters develop at the top of tall stalks, and long thin stamens project from four narrow flower petals. The flowers open in succession upward, and as the blossoms fade they are replaced by slender seed pods that spray outwards in all directions. The effect is certainly airy and graceful. Whether it is spidery is a matter of interpretation, but the plant is commonly called Spider Flower. Cultivated flowers bloom in shades of pink, rose, lavender, and white, though the typical species is purplish-pink. The large leaves are glossy dark green, and the stems are sticky to the touch.

As might be expected in the case of a tropical plant, the seeds are best started several weeks early in the greenhouse before they are transplanted in mid-spring. They develop quickly in warm weather, and when planted in fertile, well-drained soil, leap to four to six feet in height. Spider Flowers thrive in sun, but tolerate some shade and, despite their height, require no staking. The stems are stout and spiny, as gardeners removing them after frost in the autumn will attest. It takes a strong back to pull the stubborn roots and stem from the ground. (Once, after my Herculean effort, the roots came free suddenly, knocking me off my feet and nearly impaling me on the picket fence; fortunately, there were no witnesses.) With this warning in mind, cleomes are an ideal flower to display above that classic American fence. The bed should ideally be a wide one, however, so that a series of shorter flowers can lead up to the taller cleomes. They look as gawky as a row of knock-kneed chorus girls when planted alone in a narrow bed.

A split-rail fence, OPPOSITE, provides the perfect backdrop to display the architectural form of Spider Flower, *Cleome hassleriana*. The white form of Spider Flower, BELOW, displays the characteristic airy flower design of the delicate tracery of long stamens.

The extraordinary leaves of *Coleus blumei* are infinitely varied. They are blotched, streaked, and stippled with rich colors in fascinating patterns. The stems are square, which is characteristic of many members of the Labiatae. In a family of plants valued for aromatic foliage and the secretion of volatile oils, notably mints, thymes, sages, oregano, rosemary, and lavender, *Coleus* is only slightly aromatic. It compensates with color.

The species was introduced about 1825 from the South Seas island of Java. This is the only plant I've ever encountered that originated there. Come to think of it, the fact that Coleus is native to Java is the sum total of my knowledge about the island. (I once saw a movie about the volcano Krakatoa, but that was east of Java.)

The arrival of Coleus coincided with the bedding craze, so it was tailor-made for the Victorians. As a heat-loving tropical, it could be germinated in fashionable greenhouses; an annual that didn't require such care was considered common. (Wealthy Victorians often judged a plant by the energy expended to produce it, especially when it wasn't their energy that was being expended.) Plants could be pinched and trimmed to a uniform height, which was necessary for the bedding schemes. Peter Henderson wrote in 1890 that Coleus were commonly planted for "ribbon gardening, massing, or any situation where striking effect is wanted." He told how, "From the original species many varieties, remarkable for their beautiful foliage, have been produced by florists." Other species, such as

Coleus blumei Labiatae

COLEUS

ABOVE, *Coleus blumei* glows in a shaded bed. Deeper-toned Coleus, BELOW, were often used in ribbon beds. A fanciful arrangement, OPPOSITE, uses Coleus, pokeberry, asarum berries, and lamium.

C. pumilus from Ceylon, were probably used in breeding. Hybridists had a field day, and the tints of green, red, maroon, yellow, purple, and brown could be endlessly varied. The most impressive types could be propagated by cuttings, so that thousands of identical plants could be lined in rows. Coleus also prospered equally well in full sun as in shade, as well as in the conservatory or parlor.

Cultural routines for *C. blumei* vary little from the nineteenth century. Its seeds and cuttings thrive best in warm greenhouses. Coleus are usually planted in moist shady beds, for there are fewer choices for gardeners there, but they thrive in sun if enough water is furnished. Seedlings set out during cool weather will often stunt, and Coleus have no tolerance for even a degree of frost. Between late May and early June, where in most areas the night temperatures remain at least above 40°F, is the earliest time advisable for moving the plants outdoors. Gardeners in the mildest climates, something like that in Java, I suppose, sometimes grow Coleus into small shrubs. Cuttings from special plants are easily rooted, and many gardeners bring pot-grown specimens indoors in the winter. Leggy old stems are frequently cut back to promote bushiness.

Formal gardens feature Coleus to advantage, but they can provide an accent in less structured ones. Plants rarely exceed two feet, so clumps may enliven shady areas after spring bulbs and perennials have finished their show. The leaves are very handsome played against fronds of ferns. The darker varieties, with russet and burgundy tones, are effective when planted at the feet of scarlet Bee Balm, *Monarda di-*

dyma, or with the silver leaves of Dead-nettle, *Lamium maculatum.*

Coleus are a good choice for containers, where the foliage harmonizes with blooming annuals like impatiens, begonias, and fuchsias. Coleus do bloom, of course, with tiny blue flowers clustered along stems held above the leaves. The standard advice is to cut them off. This smacks of a deep-seated Victorian prejudice, and to my mind is totally unwarranted. It is high time to shed the dictates of nineteenth-century regimentation. The flowers are airy little wands that break the monotony of the foliage, and their blue coloring underscores the leaves' deep tones. The scientific name is derived from the Greek *koleos,* a sheath, which refers to the way the bottom of the stamens or anther threads are combined. It takes excellent eyesight to discover this, but those who remove the flowers never will.

Larkspurs have been grown since the times of the Pharaohs. Ancient people valued them not for the flowers, but for the seeds that were thought to destroy body vermin and ward off scorpions. Many years later that theory lost all credibility after Gerard scoffed at it. He warned that any account of the power of "Larks heele" to cause scorpions "to be without force or strength to hurt, insomuch that they cannot move . . ." was "not worth the reading." Many species of the buttercup tribe, of which larkspurs are members, are poisonous, and it is often claimed that no insects will touch them—but that has never deterred slugs, rabbits, or scorpions.

Larkspur was formerly classified as an annual *Delphinium*, but is now correctly called *Consolida*, an ancient Latin name for an unidentified plant. The nectaries of the flower are hidden behind the petals in a spur, the appearance of which suggested a bird's foot to early gardeners. The flowers also went by the names of Larks Claw, Larks Toe, and Knight's Spur. For many years it was believed that only bees with long "tongues" could reach the nectar hidden deep within the spur. Later it was discovered that wily short-tongued bees sometimes would pierce the spur from the outside. This is a coup for the bees, but circumvents pollination of the flowers.

Consolida ambigua is the Branching Larkspur. Native to the Mediterranean region, it was grown in England by 1572 at the latest. Larkspur was used to treat cuts and sores; the Latin *consolida* means to heal or fill in (old herbals often spoke of the

Consolida **Ranunculaceae**

Consolida ambigua BRANCHING LARKSPUR

Consolida orientalis ROCKET LARKSPUR

power of a plant to "fill in" a wound.) The flowers are usually blue, but can also be pink or white. This changeable trait is described by the binomial *ambigua*. It was believed that the juice of the flowers applied to the eyes could improve failing sight. French botanist J. Pitton de Tournenfort wrote in 1700, "nay, some say, that even the constant looking on them will have that effect. . . ." This may have been considered as a genuine sight for sore eyes.

Consolida orientalis is a wildflower of southeastern Europe, and was introduced to British soil in 1573. Just twenty-five years later it was a common weed in corn fields. Some versions of classical legends tell that the flowers sprang from the blood of Ajax, terror of the Trojans. Disappointed with the division of the spoils after a battle, the enraged warrior attacked a flock of sheep, wounding several. When he came to his senses, Ajax was so ashamed he turned his sword on himself. Similar stories claim the same origin for hyacinths. (Whichever is true, his blood was blue.) The cultivated flowers are commonly called Rocket Larkspurs for their tall, dense flower spikes. Sir Thomas Hanmer described them in 1659, claiming, "Some kinds grow two or three yards high, and have stalkes set so thicke with flowers that the stalkes are not to bee seene." Either Sir Thomas exaggerated a little, or he had some mighty powerful fertilizer. Rocket Larkspurs rarely exceed four feet in height. They figure prominently in the parentage of modern hybrid delphiniums.

The two species of larkspur are remarkably similar, although *C. orientalis* does not branch like *C. ambigua*, and its spurs are less noticeable. Flowers bloom in clear

An informal bouquet of Larkspur, Honeysuckle, Queen Anne's Lace, and roses, OPPOSITE, graces a vase. Self-sown *Consolida ambigua*, ABOVE, blooms.

shades of deep blue, violet, lavender, rose, pink, and white. Ample water and fertile, well-drained soil are necessary for Larkspurs to attain their normal four-foot height, although some forms barely exceed a foot. They grow best in full sun, although in areas with high summer heat they will benefit from some afternoon shade. Consolida is considered a hardy annual, in that seeds can be sown in late autumn or early spring and the young seedlings will withstand frost. They are difficult to transplant, but by no means impossible. Larkspurs are self-seeding, and can perpet-

uate themselves for years. Showy masses of the flowers in some gardens are descendants of seeds sown a half-century before.

The flowering spikes are exceptionally graceful in the garden and in bouquets. If they are cut before they reach maturity, and hung in bunches in a cool basement, the flowers may be dried for winter decoration. Brilliant orange Pot Marigold, *Calendula officinalis*, is a classic companion for vivid blue larkspur in the garden, as are crimson or pink roses, daisies, and golden coreopsis, but all of them should not necessarily be situated in the same border.

The derivation of this plant's name is from the Greek *kosmos*, meaning beautiful. How refreshing to find a name so succinct and appropriate. That it is both singular and plural, like moose and sheep, as well as being the common name, makes *Cosmos* highly unusual in the plant kingdom (*Coleus* also shares this distinction). The specific epithet *bipinnatus* refers to the feather-like arrangement of the leaves.

Seeds of Cosmos were collected in Mexico late in the eighteenth century by Dr. Martin Sessé y Lacasta and José Mociño. Charles III of Spain had commissioned expeditions to investigate the natu-

Cosmos bipinnatus Compositae

COSMOS

Stunning clumps of grasses, including Miscanthus sinensis *'Zebrinus' and* Pennisetum alopecuroides, OPPOSITE, *are enhanced by airy white* Cosmos. *Madly-blooming* Cosmos, BELOW, *spill over clipped hedges.*

ral resources of his dominions. This one was beset with problems, not the least being travelling conditions—Mociño's plea that the Spanish government export camels to Mexico went unheeded—but these paled in comparison with the earthquake, two volcanic eruptions, and the outbreak of leprosy that confronted the explorers. Seeds from the expedition reached Spain, and the Marchioness of Bute, whose husband was the English ambassador at Madrid at the time, introduced Cosmos to English horticulture in 1799.

After all that trouble, sadly to say, it was not well received. The flowers were lovely but barely managed to bloom by the first frost. England was not an ideal climate for the plant since it needs real heat to come

into perfection. Gardeners tended to be too kind to Cosmos; planting it in fertile loam encouraged lush foliage but few flowers. American seedsmen selected early-maturing plants, which helped, but there was an unlikely twist to the story. It was the poorest gardeners, or at least those with the poorest soil, that achieved the greatest success with Cosmos and made it famous. Even the most negligent gardener could boast of a superb stand of Cosmos.

The word stand is apropos; plants often reach five feet by summer's end. Starting in July, branched stems are produced over finely dissected leaves. Clusters of simple daisy-like flowers, nearly four inches across, bloom on each stem in shades of pink, deep rose, and white. There is no point in lining Cosmos in rows, for they are quite at their best when seedlings are allowed to volunteer in random patterns,

or the gardener imitates such an effect.

This is another plant that looks ever-so-natural billowing over a picket fence. The Cosmos in my garden do just that, mingling with *Artemisia frigida* 'Silver King', *Rosa rugosa*, and wine-pink Coneflower, *Echinacea purpurea.* If the flowers are cut

when they first open they will last for a week or more in water. Best of all, it is nearly impossible to arrange them badly. Take fifteen stems or more, strip the lower leaves, and plunk them into the handiest container, be it cut crystal or canning jar. The result will be unstudied elegance.

A profusion of flowers from a fine stand of Cosmos lends an airy touch to a formally-designed annual garden, where they are segregated from pelargoniums by a low hedge, OPPOSITE. Fresh-picked blossoms of *C. bipinnatus* need little arranging to make an appealing display in a collection of crockery, ABOVE.

Dianthus barbatus Caryophyllaceae

SWEET WILLIAM

Sweet William, *Dianthus barbatus*, is an old inhabitant of the flower garden. A native to southern Europe, it was likely introduced to England by Carthusian monks in the twelfth century. Traditionally, it has been supposed that the name referred to William the Conqueror, but it is much more likely that it originally was called Sweet Saint William for St. William of Aquitaine.

When Henry VIII had a new garden planted at Hampton Court in 1533, Sweet Williams were purchased in bulk, at the going rate of threepence the bushel. They collected the folk names of Velvet Williams, Bloomy-downs, London Tufts, Colminiers, and Col-me-neers, the latter stemming from the word "coll," meaning an embrace. Col-me-neer would appear to have been a rather romantic name, and highly appropriate for the fragrant bunched flower heads. Herbalist John Parkinson wrote in the early seventeenth cen-

tury that the speckled variety "is termed by our English Gentlewomen London Pride." The name was a good one, but it became more closely associated with *Saxifraga umbrosa* (which, incidentally, was originally called Prince's Feather, a name usually reserved today for *Amaranthus hypochondriacus.*)

Sweet William was highly esteemed in Elizabethan times for, as Gerard wrote, "its beauty to deck up the bosoms of the beautiful, and garlands, and crowns for pleasure." The beautiful may not have needed any such decking up, but its fragrant flowers were especially valued in the days before daily baths became commonplace.

When William, Duke of Cumberland, led the English army to victory over the Scottish clans in 1745, there was rejoicing throughout the land. With the Jacobite rebellion crushed, an unattributed poet wrote a verse commemorating the day, a passage of which reads:

Since the Duke's victorious blows
The lily thistle and the rose
All droop and fade, all die away
Sweet William only rules the day.

The Scots retorted by naming one of their most obnoxious weeds "Stinking Billy." The famous "sticks and stones" taunt has, unfortunately, not been attributed to the Duke of Cumberland.

For a flower so long grown in England, and especially one probably associated with a saint, it is remarkable to find that Sweet William had no use in medicine or cooking. It appears to have been grown for pleasure alone. It was not particularly fashionable, in any age, for it was already considered old-fashioned. Nevertheless, Sweet William has always had a legion of admirers. Peter Henderson wrote one hundred years ago of his fondness, for "it sports into endless varieties of color, white, pink, purple, crimson and scarlet self colors, and many sorts of variously edged, eyed or spotted. There are also many beautiful double-flowered varieties," which, he noted, "can only be perpetuated by division or cutting." Most of the doubles are extinct, but Sweet William is still to be found in all the old colors.

D. barbatus is usually grown as an annual or biennial, but under favorable conditions it will persist longer. Its seeds are often sown in early summer, and the young plants are carried over the winter in cold frames, or moved to permanent positions in the garden in autumn and mulched for winter protection. Rosettes of lace-shaped leaves produce stems topped by flat closely-packed clusters of flowers. The blossoms of Sweet William carry a spicy clove fragrance similar to the aroma of carnations and pinks, which are closely related.

Sweet William is adaptable to many situations and grows well in sun or partial-shade with normal watering, but fares poorly in acidic soil. Plants bloom most generously in spring and early summer, but will sometimes flower well into autumn. Volunteer seedlings are common and need to be thinned to allow enough room for proper development. As befits this quintessential old-fashioned favorite, it is best planted cottage-style. Clumps of multi-colored Sweet William are charming beneath the arching branches of roses.

In 1901, Alice Morse Earle recalled "the rioting Sweet Williams . . . bathed in glowing sunlight and color," as they are still found, OPPOSITE and BELOW.

Flowers have long been associated with fairies. The little people dressed themselves in cloaks of petals, slept in flowers, and sat on mushrooms. The mottled markings of the Foxglove, like those on butterflies and the tails of pheasants—on which fairies stole rides—showed where elves had placed their fingers. Foxglove may have originally been called Folk's Glove, named for the wee folks. Properly known as *Digitalis purpurea*, the Latin name for the plant itself suggests gloves or fingers; *digitus* means finger. A legend neatly explains that mischievous fairies gave the blossoms to the fox, that he might soften the tread of his toes as he prowled about the chicken coop.

Foxglove may also be derived from Foxes-gleow; a gleow was an old musical instrument with an arch that supported bells of graduating sizes, not unlike the structure of the flower spike itself. The plant is called Fox Bells and Fox Music in Scandinavian countries. Not everyone believed in fairies or musically-inclined foxes. In some localities in the British Isles it was called Ditch-tail and Floppydock, and, across the Channel, the French called it, of all things, Virgin's Glove.

Foxgloves are native to Europe, including Britain. Gardeners have transported them to the far corners of the earth, and they now grow wild in the Andes and in New Zealand, where some despise them as noxious weeds. Early herbalists recommended Foxglove to treat fever and liver trouble, as well as a mysterious ailment known as the "King's Evil." The Welsh applied the plant externally for scrofulous complaints; its family name, Scrophulariaceae, alludes to this use.

This plant can either kill or cure. All of its parts are poisonous, but the drug digitalin used in the treatment of heart disease, is extracted from the leaves. Remarkably, the old herbalists never discovered this genuine virtue; Dr. William

FOXGLOVE

*S*elf-sown spikes of **F**oxglove, *D*igitalis *purpurea*, growing at an old gravesite, ABOVE, underscore the beneficial—and poisonous—nature of the plant. **O**ld stories told that fairies hid or napped in the purple blossoms of **F**oxglove, OPPOSITE, flowering at woodland's edge in June.

Withering of Birmingham, England, discovered Foxglove's beneficial properties and used it to treat patients with dropsy about 1780. This treatment became widespread throughout Europe, and apothecaries in Paris painted the image of foxgloves on doorposts and walls.

Digitalis purpurea also possessed a more sinister reputation. Witches' Thimble and Bloody-man's Fingers were country names signifying its dark side. The plant was sacred to the Druids, it was whispered, for the purple flowers resembled the high priest's mitre and, worst of all, it bloomed at the time of the midsummer sacrifice. Other flowers were in bloom at this time as well, but it is the poisonous ones that are apt to become associated with deadly doings. Parents have always used frightful images to keep children away from danger; this should never be underestimated in attempting to understand folklore.

Flowers of *Digitalis* are typically pale purple, as the specific epithet *purpurea* implies, but occasionally white ones are found in the wild. These have been used to create hybrids in various shades of pink and apricot. The irregular dark spots inside the flower throat—easily imagined to have been left by fairies—are encircled by thin white rings. The flower spikes usually grow to five feet or more, and bloom in early summer. Foxgloves are biennial, and once planted, will usually seed themselves. Plants grow in all types of soil, but are commonly found at the edge of woods in moist places. By re-creating an environment where a Druid would feel comfortable, the gardener may successfully grow a fine stand of Foxgloves.

Digitalis purpurea
Scrophulariaceae

Dolichos lablab Leguminosae

 It is always fascinating to discover the country of origin of a plant. It may be startling to learn that the Hyacinth Bean, so closely associated with informal gardens in America, is actually a native of Egypt. It has been grown since ancient days in tropical lands of the Old World for food and forage. *Dolichos lablab* was introduced to Western horticulture in 1818, and was known for a time as the Egyptian Bean or Bonavist. The scientific name, which for all the world sounds like a dish from a Mexican-Swedish restaurant, means long, and refers to the vine's long, twining shoots. Neither a hyacinth nor a bean, *Dolichos* was the ancient Greek name for a species of pea, and it is possible they could have known this one. The vine is locally called Lablab in tropical Africa, and in a rare case, the common name became part of the scientific one.

Peter Henderson wrote in 1890 that "the pods and seeds are eatable (sic), and, in some cases, the roots." Most gardeners grow the Hyacinth Bean for the sweet scent of its flowers. They are shaped with the trademark wing petals of the Leguminosae, the pea family.

The purple flowers, usually an inch wide, are arranged on long spikes and begin to bloom in midsummer. The effect is not unlike that of a wisteria, although the flowers do not droop. They will continue to bloom until cut down by frost. The clear blossoms are complemented by the dusky purple-tinted stems and three- to six-inch leaflets that are displayed in sets of three. The flowers are followed by curved pods containing black seeds. Henderson mentioned a white-flowering variety as if it was as common as the purple, but it is rarely seen today.

The vines are perennial in their native habitat, where they can easily grow to thirty feet. Even in temperate climates, they often reach ten feet and can cover a trellis in short order; the Hyacinth Bean climbs by twining. It was occasionally grown in conservatories in the nineteenth century. As a tropical plant, Hyacinth Bean responds to summer heat and grows poorly in chilly areas. Gardeners often germinate the seeds in a warm greenhouse. A good rule of thumb is to transplant seedlings when it is safe to plant tomatoes. Seedlings are notoriously difficult to transplant, so it is advisable to start them in peat pots to avoid root disturbance.

Hyacinth Bean is an excellent choice for gardeners where intense summer heat precludes the possibility of growing Sweet Peas successfully. The vines are especially lovely when they are intertwined with morning glories. The purple flower spikes contrast with the trumpet-shaped morning glories, and are equally effective with blue, red, or white varieties. The advantage, of course, is that *Dolichos lablab* stays open for the entire day. Similarly, Hyacinth Bean can be planted at the feet of spring-flowering shrub roses or climbers, where they will provide flowers long after the roses have finished their mad flush.

Upright sprays of Hyacinth Bean, *Dolichos lablab*, intertwine with Morning Glory, ABOVE.

HYACINTH BEAN

Fuchsia × *hybrida* Onagraceae

LADY'S EARDROPS

The pendant flowers of *Fuchsia* × *hybrida*, ABOVE, enchanted Victorians. The plants are often trained as upright standards, OPPOSITE, and brought outdoors for summer display.

One of the most charming stories about the introduction of a plant is told about the fuchsia. According to the tale, a widow received the first of these plants, *F. coccinea*, from her sailor son after a voyage to South America about 1785. An enterprising nurseryman, James Lee, spotted the pendulous flowers on her windowsill and offered to buy the plant. She refused to part with her son's gift, but Lee persuaded her to allow him to take the plant and propagate it, later returning with two fine new plants. It has been suggested that, as lovely as the story is, it was probably a ruse that obscured the truth—Kew Gardens had recently brought the fuchsia into cultivation under glass, and some light fingers had pinched a cutting. In horticulture, nothing remains exclusive for long.

Even so, the fuchsia has a fascinating early history. Charles Plumier, a botanist and missionary, lived in Haiti during the last decade of the seventeenth century. He discovered the new genus and named it for Leonhard Fuchs, a German naturalist and professor of medicine. Father Plumier published his findings in 1703, describing and illustrating what he called *Fuchsia triphylla flore coccinea* (Linnaeus dropped the last two words in his first edition of *Species Plantarum*). No specimens of the plant ever arrived in Europe, and many botanists doubted its existence entirely, for it was not seen again for 170 years. American Thomas Hogg finally secured its seed in 1873 near Santo Domingo.

Meanwhile, other species from South and Central America had been discovered

by plant hunters and introduced during the first half of the nineteenth century. Hybridists set to work, and many new cultivars were ushered in during the Victorian era. The conservatories and new glass houses provided a congenial home for these tropical plants, and the Victorians were enchanted by the drooping flowers. The plants were trained into whimsical shapes for exhibition, and were especially favored for tiered arrangements. They were called Lady's Eardrops, referring to the earrings of elegant women, but the name sounds medicinal instead. Fuchsia—the color—was named for the flowers.

Some of the species proved to be hardy—notably *F. magellanica*, which is collected near the Straits of Magellan—and are grown in mild climates as shrubs. Even the tender varieties can be grown as small trees, shuttled seasonally between the open air and the greenhouse. Of the estimated fifteen hundred hybrids grown during the height of the fuchsia fashion, very few remain today. The First World War spelled doom for many, as growing vegetable crops became the priority, and many young gardeners went off to battle. A re-

vival in interest during this century has led to the creation of many new hybrids that echo those grown in the past. These can trace their ancestry to the golden days of the Victorian infatuation with fuchsias, when both rich and poor admired them. Thomas Hardy considered the congruity of one such Victorian's preoccupation in "The Lodging House Fuchsias":

> Mrs Master's fuchsias hung
> Higher and broader, and brightly swung,
>   Bell-like, more and more
> Over the narrow garden-path,
> Giving the passer a sprinkle-bath
>   in the morning.

> She put up with their pushful ways,
> And made us tenderly lift their sprays,
>   Going to her door:
> But when her funeral had to pass
> They cut back all the flowery mass
>   In the morning.

Fuchsias are most often grown in hanging baskets, the better to appreciate the arching sprays of flowers. Four sepals flare from a slender tube. The sepals encase the corolla of petals which dangles like a petticoat, and the delicate stamens and longer stigma hang from this cloaking. Flowers classified as single have only four petals, and doubles have eight or more. The petals and sepals may be of different colors, such as white and pink, or may be of similar colors. Red, rose, lavender, purple, white, and pink hues predominate, but some species are coral and orange. Gardeners often situate their plants in shady spots protected from drying winds, although in mild climates they grow perfectly well in sun with ample moisture.

Gomphrena globosa is native to India, and tradition holds that it was brought to Europe by Alexander the Great. It is thought to be the Amaranth of the poets who saw in its long-lasting flowers a symbol of immortality or, at least, undying love. The Greeks wore the flowers of Globe Amaranth at funerals, as Homer describes in his account of the burial of Achilles. The flowers became popular throughout the Mediterranean region. The churches in Portugal were adorned with them. Spanish shepherdesses would weave them with Laurel to fashion crowns and chaplets—one could probably spot a shepherdess a mile away. *Gomphrena globosa* first flowered in England in 1714.

The name *Gomphrena* stems from the Greek *gomphos*, a club, alluding to the shape of the flowers, while *globosa* means spherical. The flower heads resemble those of clover, and are generally seen in white, pink, and magenta shades. The flower heads have a papery texture even while fresh. When picked and dried properly, they retain their coloring well and are useful for dried arrangements. Quite the best of annuals for enlivening the border from midsummer until frost, the plants grow to ten inches in height, and by late summer they are smothered with blossoms.

Clumps of the magenta form make effective accents among a pastel combination of Queen Anne's Lace, *Daucus carota*, Pearly Everlasting, *Anaphalis margaritacea*, and Pur-

The colors of *G. globosa* are effective together, OPPOSITE. Globe Amaranths brighten a bouquet of wildflowers, ABOVE. *G. globosa* pokes through double petunias and Black-eyed Susans, BELOW.

Gomphrena globosa
Amaranthaceae

ple Coneflower, *Echinacea purpurea*. The white and pale pink contrast effectively with *Campanula carpatica* and *Coreopsis verticillata* 'Moonbeam'. Gardeners who are loathe to plant mixtures of annuals—preferring uniform clear colors—may be surprised how smashing the mixture of all three colors of Globe Amaranth can be in informal designs. The flowers serve well in mixed container plantings as well.

Globe Amaranth is a slow starter. The seeds need to be germinated in the greenhouse several months before they are transplanted to the garden. Peter Henderson was familiar with the slow development of the plants in the late Victorian age. His 1890 *Handbook of Plants* recommended the following: "The seeds are slow to germinate, and should be sown in March in a hot-bed or in seed pans in the green-house. The plants will be greatly benefitted by pricking out, or re-potting before planting time in the open border. With this treatment single plants can be made to produce several hundred flowers."

Because the plants require time and the heat of summer to come on strongly, they rarely catch the eye of the gardener struck with spring fever. Home gardeners seldom achieve success by sowing the seed *in situ*, and the plants are not often known as self-sowers from the previous year. Gardeners often rely on their local nursery to provide healthy young seedlings for early summer transplanting. *Gomphrena globosa* thrives in full sun in ordinary soil, and copes well with heat and tolerates a degree of drought.

Of all the exotic new flowers found by European explorers in South America, the Sunflower was the most impressive. The Incas had already bred *Helianthus annuus*, probably of Central American origin, into a towering stalk topped by enormous golden flowers. Designs of the flower were carved into temples, and gold emblems of the flower of the sun god adorned the ever-popular Virgins of the Sun.

The seeds were quickly sent back to Spanish botanists (probably with a cautionary note to plant them and stand back). *H. annuus* was described by Dr. Nicholas Monardes in 1569 in the first book published about the flora of the New World. Translated into English under the gleeful title *Joyfull news out of the newe founde worlde*, it heralds the "Hearbe of the Sunne" as "a straunge flower, for it casteth out the greatest flowers, and the most perticulars that ever hath been seen, for it is greater than a greate Platter or Dishe. . . ."

Gardeners all over Europe engaged in an informal game of one-upsmanship, something like "anything you can grow, I can grow higher." Gerard claimed, "It hath risen up to the height of fourteene foote in my garden, where one flower was in weight three pound and two ounces. . . ." Crispin de Pass boasted of one Sunflower that "sown in the Royal Garden at Madrid in Spain, it grew to twenty four feet." Not to be outdone, the Italians, perhaps inspired by stories of Jacco and the Beanstalk, insisted that a plant in Padua attained forty feet.

The plant was dubbed *Helianthus*, from

Helianthus annuus Compositae

SUNFLOWER

Goldfinches and schoolboys savor the seeds, arranged in a honeycomb pattern, of giant *Sunflower,*
Helianthus annuus, OPPOSITE ABOVE and BELOW, that commonly grows to ten feet or more. The state flower
of Kansas, ABOVE, likely had help becoming established on the plains by west-bound settlers.

the Greek *helios*, the sun, and *anthos*, a flower. The French called it *tournesol*, turn with the sun. It was thought that the giant flower heads followed the sun, facing eastward at dawn and to the west at sundown. It seems no one ever actually verified this fact by actual observation, but it was widely accepted. The biochemical propensity of plants to turn towards a light source is called phototropism. It should be noted that when they first bloom, the huge seed-bearing cultivars do exhibit such signs, inclining their heads towards the sun. This inspired a gruesome fable, the moral of which escapes me, about a Sunflower that twisted its head right off. The Victorians were experts at moralizing. It should come as no surprise that in 1850 the Reverend R. Warner would include the Sunflower in his poems pondering "Floral Decay: emblematical of man's mortal condition."

> *And, thou,* Bold plant, *that* lov'st *the sun!*
> (Emblem of human vanity:)
> *Shalt, soon, thy* measured course *have run!*
> *For,* thou, *alas!* must shortly *die!*

The cheerful Reverend Warner wrote six other verses about the Sunflower but they need not be printed here.

After the novelty waned—it's difficult to incorporate a forty-foot flower into the border gracefully—gardeners began to search for other uses for the Sunflower. The Incas had, of course, made use of the fibers, seed, and flower petals, from which they extracted a yellow dye. The pith of the stalk is said to be one of the lightest materials known, and some later inventors experimented with making life jackets from it. A single flower head contains as many as two thousand seeds, rich in protein and oil, that Alice Coats noted were "particularly acceptable to turkeys, parrots, pheasants and Russians." Sunflowers are grown commercially in many parts of the world for the oil. It is said that those who chew the seeds, which contain calcium, have fewer dental problems. (If only my sixth-grade teacher had known this.)

The multiflowered forms of Sunflowers—akin to the original wild flower—have much smaller blossoms.

Garden forms have been bred with pale yellow petals, two-toned combinations, or deeper reddish tones. The latter stem from a single red-flowering sport found near Boulder, Colorado, at the beginning of the century. Tales are told of westward-travelling Mormons who scattered Sunflower seeds so that other settlers could follow a trail of golden flowers in succeeding years. Sunflowers are synonymous with the American Great Plains where they have once again become wild.

Multi-branched Sunflowers, OPPOSITE, add country charm to a contemporary bouquet. Varieties of *Helianthus annuus* grow quickly from seeds to five feet or more in height, ABOVE.

Heliotropium arborescens is unique among its own family—which includes Borage, Comfrey, Forget-me-not, and Alkanet—in possessing a delightful fragrance. Heliotrope was given the country name Cherry Pie on account of this scent, though the parallel is difficult to draw. Somewhere between the perfumes of lilac and daphne—at least to my nose—it is a fresh, sweet scent that seems to appeal to most people.

Heliotropium is derived from the Greek *helios*, the sun, and *trope*, to turn, in the mistaken belief that the flower heads turned to follow the sun. It may have been a little easier in the past to believe that the golden discs of Sunflowers could perform such a feat, but the upfacing clusters of tiny Heliotrope blossoms sit so primly erect on top their stems that it is difficult to imagine them swaying with the advance of the sun through the day. Gerard also was bothered by the inaccuracy, and suggested that perhaps the name had been misinterpreted. He suggested, rather unconvincingly, that the Heliotrope was so named, not "because it is turned about at the daily motion of the sunne, but by reason it flowereth in the summer Solstice, at which time the sunne being farthest gone from the aequinoctial circle, returneth to the same." Even so, the legend persisted, eventually working its way into discussions of morality. An eighteenth-century English minister urged his flock, "Let us all be heliotropes (if I may use the expression) to the Sun of Righteousness."

Some herbalists employed the flowers as a remedy for warts and gout, although it had far greater value as an ingredient in perfumes. The flowers were also harvested for a lozenge that was touted as being "of great service in clergyman's sore throat."

Heliotrope was discovered in the Peruvian Andes by French botanist Joseph de Jussieu, who smelled its fragrance on the breeze before he found it. He sent seed to the Jardin du Roi in Paris, where it first flowered in 1740. The plant is a tall perennial in its native land, as the binomial *arborescens*, meaning tree-like, describes. More compact forms were produced in short order so that it could be featured in bedding schemes. The flowers of the species are pale lavender, but selection produced deeper purple and rosy violet tones, as well as white. The flower is most closely associated with Victorian sensibilities—nosegays, courtship, and such. In the language of flowers which flourished in the nineteenth century, Heliotrope symbolized devotion. The flower was a pleasure, but a rather chaste and wholesome one. An unattributed Victorian poem sung its praise:

> *There is a flower whose modest eye*
> *Is turned with looks of light and love,*
> *Who breathes her softest, sweetest sigh,*
> *Whene'er the sun is bright above.*

Heliotropes are easily grown from seed started during the late winter months in the greenhouse. Planted out when the soil and nights are warm, they begin to bloom in midsummer. The leaves are deep green, often with a purple cast. A sunny site and generous watering serve them well. Modern hybrids have lost a degree of the cherished scent. The most fragrant individuals may be saved and propagated by cuttings. Heliotrope provides a most welcome sweet fragrance in a sunroom or conservatory during wintertime.

Heliotropium arborescens
Boraginaceae

CHERRY PIE

Forget-me-nots, *Myosotis scorpioides*, poke through fragrant flower heads
of Cherry Pie, *Heliotropium arborescens*, OPPOSITE. Gertrude Jekyll admired the
soft tint of the flowers of *H. arborescens*, ABOVE.

Impatiens balsamina Balsaminaceae

The Balsam of yesteryear, *Impatiens balsamina*, has been largely overshadowed by its near relative, the hybrid impatiens that is among the top-selling nursery plants for seasonal displays. Balsam was, in all likelihood, introduced to English gardens by traders from the East Indies before 1600; it is remarkable that it has been cultivated for nearly four hundred years. Both Gerard and Parkinson grew it, and Turner's herbal features a drawing of it.

The flowers were favorites in American colonial gardens, and continued as popular plants until the turn of this century, when they fell from favor. Peter Henderson held an obvious affection for Balsam, saying, "It is one of the showiest and most popular of summer flowers, blooming as does till the advent of frost." He details the French camellia-flowered varieties and the German rose-flowered kinds, and exclaims, "The spotted varieties form a class by themselves, and are justly regarded as among the most brilliant ornaments of the garden. . . ."

Impatiens is Latin for impatient, an apt description of the sudden discharge of seed from the ripe seed capsules. Children and most gardeners, if pressed on the subject, will admit they find great fun in touching the seed pods and provoking the explosive release. The common names Touch-me-not and Jumping Betty relate this silly pleasure. The binomial *balsamina*, which means "bearing balsam," was chosen because it was originally thought to yield the aromatic resin used in medicine and perfume; but the blossoms and leaves are without scent. Native women of the East Indies

BALSAM

Stalks of Balsam highlight an annual garden of old-fashioned favorites, OPPOSITE, including Sweet Alyssum, *Lobularia maritima*, and Tickseed, *Coreopsis tinctoria*. ABOVE, Balsam flowers are displayed in the leaf axils of the thick stems. Few flowers rivalled Balsam for popularity in colonial American gardens, BELOW.

formerly extracted a dye from the flowers to paint their fingernails—a handy tip for do-it-yourself lady gardeners.

Balsam grows to several feet on thick fleshy stems studded with pointed, finely-serrated leaves. The flowers clustered in the leaf axils along the stem are doubled and very pretty, displaying shades of pink, white, plum, and scarlet. The spotted ones are still to be found and, amazingly, come true from seed. Green-fingered clergyman William Hanbury, writing in 1769, told that *I. balsamina* was "reckoned an annual of the first class, and . . . has occasioned much emulation among Gardeners to show it in its greatest perfection. . . ." The perfect ones must have been marvellous, for the flowers of some were described to be "as large as middling roses." These were called, during the eighteenth century, Immortal Eagle Flowers, for reasons unknown. Modern dwarf varieties are but a shadow of Balsam's true beauty.

As befits its tropical origin, Balsam is best raised from seed in the greenhouse and transplanted when the weather has settled. Gerard had no such luxury, and he advised that, "They must be sowen in the beginning of April in a bed of hot horse-dung . . . and replanted abroad from the said bed into the most hot and fertill place of the garden at such time as they have gotten three leaves a peece." Where summers are warmer than those enjoyed by Gerard, the seedlings can be planted in any location that receives a half day's sun or more. Unlike hybrid impatiens, *I. balsamina* fails to thrive in shaded areas. The Balsam plants in my garden generally thumb their noses at my careful pains, seeding themselves with abandon.

 The original Sweet Pea was an unassuming wildflower from Sicily and southern Italy. Its small maroon and blue blossoms, just two to a stem, were not considered great beauties of the floral kingdom, though it did possess an exquisite fragrance. A description of it was first published in 1697 by an Italian botanist-priest, Franciscus Cupani. It was classified as *Lathyrus odoratus*; the genus name was Greek for pea, and *odoratus* means scented. Two years later, Father Cupani sent seed of the new scented pea to Dr. Robert Uvedale, the headmaster of a grammar school in England. A keen gardener, Uvedale was enchanted by the Sweet Pea's perfume, and shared the seeds with friends.

By 1772, the seeds were available for sale, and nurseryman Thomas Fairchild recommended them in his *City Gardiner* to Londoners, saying, "The sweet-scented Pea makes a beautiful Plant, having Spikes of Flowers of a red and blue Colour." He attempted to describe the scent as "somewhat like Honey and a little tending to the Orange-flower Smell." Fairchild's description seems as close as any, for scents are difficult to put into words. Whatever it was, the Sweet Pea caught on with the public, although by 1850 it was still to be found in just a few colors.

The trouble was that the flowers are self-fertile with resultingly few chances for cross-pollination. Natural selection was slow; hybridists had to force the issue to induce color breaks. The most successful was Henry Eckford, who spent thirty years improving the Sweet Pea. Not only did he improve the shape, substance, and size of the flowers, as well as distill a palette of pastels from the original maroon and blue, but he coaxed the flower stems to bloom with four flowers instead of two. When the Bi-Centenary Sweet Pea Exhibition was held at the Crystal Palace in 1900, more than half of the 264 varieties shown were Eckford's.

By that time, no dinner table or wedding bouquet in England or America was complete without Sweet Peas. Rare was the garden that did not sport a fence or trellis of them. Teepee structures of brush and thin wooden stakes were erected for the twining vines to climb. Even city dwellers could enjoy the flowers, for they were raised by the thousands under glass. Celia Thaxter conjured a romantic notion from her island garden, writing:

> *Across the little garden comes the breeze,*
> *Bows all its cups of flame, and brings to me*
> *Its breath of mignonette and bright sweet-peas,*
> *With drowsy murmurs from the encircling sea.*

Lathyrus odoratus is as easy to grow as edible garden peas, preferring a stiff loam in a sunny site with ample water. Extensive breeding has all but ruined the scent the Sweet Pea was loved for in the first place. In search of bigger blooms and ever more ruffles, Sweet Pea fanatics nearly bred the scent out of the plant in the first half of this century. Fortunately, many of the older lines have survived—saved by home gardeners for generations—and have once again been offered to the public, as well as contributing to the breeder's gene pool. The older varieties, more closely related to the wildflowers of Sicily, are not only more fragrant, but show more tolerance to heat.

Sweet Pea, *Lathyrus odoratus*, has traditionally been grown on teepees of stiff bamboo rods and brush, ABOVE, to which the vines cling with their tendrils.

Lathyrus odoratus Leguminosae

SWEET PEA

Lavatera trimestris Malvaceae

ROSE MALLOW

 Joseph Breck's *The Young Florist* (1833) was intended to interest children in gardening. The book is essentially a play in which the extraordinarily brilliant children, Margaret and Henry, converse on all subjects horticultural, not the least being the planning of a charming circular garden. In it, the prodigies include the favorite flowers of the day, including three varieties of *Lavatera trimestris;* the children plant the seeds of white and pink Lavatera, as well as one that is "light red strip'd."

Lavatera trimestris originated in the Mediterranean region. One of the prettiest members of the mallow family, it is closely related to the Hollyhock. The cup-like flowers measure up to three inches across, and are generally seen in a pretty shade of raspberry pink with darker veining. The upright branching stems grow from three to four feet, and the lower leaves somewhat resemble those of maples.

Lavatera is a sun-loving plant and flourishes in sandy loam. It is best to sow seed in spring since transplanting is difficult but by no means impossible. As fewer gardeners during this century than ever before have grown their annuals from seed, relying on nursery stock instead, Lavatera has been seen less and less. Just a few years ago the seeds were nearly impossible to obtain in America, but lately they have enjoyed a resurgence as a new generation discovers the lovely pink flowers.

Gardeners have yet to come up with a decent common name for *Lavatera trimestris*. The scientific name honors the brothers Lavater, sixteenth-century naturalists from Zurich, while *trimestris* means "of three months" and refers to the flowering season. Three Month Mallow has never quite captured the public's imagination, and Rose Mallow, though a prettier name, could well be applied to a number of species. The oft-used common name Tree Mallow is borrowed from its bushy six-foot cousins, *L. arborea* and *L. thuringiaca*.

Like petunia, *Lavatera* may end up becoming the common name as well. Many such Latin names have been readily accepted by the public, including chrysanthemum, impatiens, delphinium, coleus, clematis, and ageratum, without any loss in their popularity. Precocious Margaret and Henry simply called the plant lavatera. Some retailers apparently feel some need to shelter us from scientific names. I once read a suggestion that the Prairie Gentian, *Eustoma grandiflorum* (also called *Lisianthus russellianus*), a wildflower from Colorado, be marketed as "Love Lizzies." I dread to think what the same promotion genius would invent for *Lavatera*.

L. trimestris grows in an informal cutting garden with cabbage, OPPOSITE. Lavatera combines gracefully with Tickseed and Balsam, ABOVE, and with *Nicotiana alata*, BELOW.

Native to southern Europe and northern Africa, *Malva sylvestris* has become naturalized in vast areas, including Great Britain and my garden. I'm not complaining. The open five-petalled flowers bloom throughout the summer on two-foot stems. As you might expect from a plant with such a wide geographic distribution, it displays great variation in color, form, and height. The variety most often seen is pale rose-lavender with conspicuous violet veining on the petals. Selected forms have a deeper color, and in some the flowers are rosy-purple and cup-shaped.

Cheese Mallow is a fitting name for this plant, because its seed heads resemble a round head of sliced cheese. *Malva sylvestris* is but one of the many Old World mallows that have been grown in gardens for many centuries. It is related to hibiscus, hollyhock, and lavatera. *Malva* is the Greek name for this group of plants, and though *sylvestris* means "of woods," Cheese mallow is more likely found in open fields, where it blooms throughout the summer.

The plant was scorned during Victorian days as a roadside weed, which, in England today, I admit that it is. Cottage gardeners have found, however, that its flowers are welcome long-blooming additions to most informal plantings. The paler forms seem to highlight other flowers most effectively, particularly the cream-and-pink bells of *Campanula punctata* and the lavender sprays of *Thalictrum aquilegifolium*.

Like so many antique annuals, it defies regimentation into bedding packs. The seeds are best sown in early spring where they are to grow. Once it is established, Cheese Mallow will return unfailingly; in milder climates the plants may survive the wintër. The seeds are too heavy to be wind-borne, so the colonies of seedlings migrate slowly around the garden. Small plants can be transplanted easily, and adapt well to pot culture. Cutting them back in late summer encourages new bloom.

I was very disappointed when I learned that its former name, *Althaea zebrina*, had been discounted. Not only was *zebrina*, meaning striped, such an apt description, but in discussing the plant in class I would mention in a deadpan manner the related species, *Althaea later*, and pause. It was a lousy pun, but a good way to gauge how many students were awake.

Malva sylvestris Malvaceae

CHEESE MALLOW

An antique biscuit box, OPPOSITE, makes a fitting container for pale and deeper-toned varieties of Cheese Mallow, *Malva sylvestris*. Cheese Mallow seeds itself throughout the garden, ABOVE. The striped flowers of *M. sylvestris*, RIGHT, inspired the old botanic name *Althaea zebrina*.

Stocks were favorites of the Elizabethans, who called them Stock-gillyflowers, for their spicy fragrance was similar to the Gillyflowers we now call carnations. The plants were distinguished by their thick stems, or "stocks," the name by which we still know them. They were also called Garnzie Violets, but the genus was renamed after Pierandrea Mattioli, a sixteenth-century Italian botanist and physician to Emperor Maximilian II.

Matthiola incana (the "h" in the name was added later—Mattioli himself did not use it) grows wild along the southwestern coasts of Europe. The flowers are pale lavender, with the four petals so typical of the Cruciferae, the Mustard family. Even by the seventeenth century, it was an old-fashioned flower of English gardens, and one on which much attention was lavished. Cultivated forms in many shades of red and purple, as well as white, were valued only when the flowers were double. Every botanist and gardener had the secret for producing doubles, which he was happy to share in great detail. Some recommended sea sand in the potting mixture and soaking the seed in brine. One fascinating eighteenth-century figure, John Hill, who

One suspects that the "unsinkable"
Molly Brown would have been charmed
by the bouquet of Stocks
and Rose of Sharon, RIGHT, on her piano.
OPPOSITE, Night-scented Stock,
M. bicornis, closes its petals at dawn.

Matthiola Cruciferae

Matthiola bicornis NIGHT-SCENTED STOCK

Matthiola incana STOCK

worked in turn as an apothecary, actor, journalist, and quack doctor, recommended the practice in 1757. Though his advice might have been taken with a grain of salt, as he was described as "in a chariot one month and in jail the next," he promised "the seeds saved from these Plants will not fail to produce the Gardener many double and very fine Flowers. . . ." He hedged his bet, however, when he admitted that the best way to produce seeds for double flowers was to "exchange them annually with some Person of integrity at a Distance," and if one's seeds failed to produce doubles for him, the worst he could do would be to send a nasty letter.

M. incana was apparently used on a limited scale in medicine. Gerard mentions this in passing, but says that it was used only by "certain Empericks and Quack-salvers, about love and lust matters, which for modestie I omit." More's the pity.

Stocks were nearly always grown as biennials. From a spring sowing during a full moon, the seedlings were frequently transplanted during three succeeding full moons, and set in the garden at Michaelmas ("dig a Hole with a Spade about as broad and deep as a Hat") for blooming the following year. The famous Brompton Stocks were raised by the nursery of London and Wise in Brompton. The so-called Ten-week Stock was an annual strain bred by weavers in northern France. It was said that each village grew only one color or variety of which they were justly proud. These figure prominently in the hybrid heritage of the annual flowers grown today.

The Night-scented Stock, *M. bicornis*, came from Greece. Its four-petalled flower folds up by day, unfurling only at dusk to release its exquisite perfume. The aroma hangs on the evening air, enveloping the garden with potent sweetness. The lavender and white blossom closes the next morning and its scent evaporates with the dawn. Night-scented Stock has been ob-

Double flowers of *M. incana*, OPPOSITE, have traditionally been preferred over the singles. *S*tocks suit farmhouse-style informality, ABOVE, planted with *Chrysanthemum weyrichii* and a carpet of *Veronica filiformis*.

served to open during an eclipse of the sun. Hermon Bourne's 1833 *Flores Poetici: The Florist's Manual* includes "the following beautiful lines, from a recent English publication, addressed to the 'Melancholy Gilliflower, which is only fragrant at night.'" The poem expressed a grave concern about the flower's feelings, and goes on for most of a page before it concludes:

> But thou dost long for holy eve,
> To shroud thee from day's piercing eye,
> Night's chilly hours alone receive
> The secret tear and perfumed sigh.

Ten-week Stock is easily raised from seed and transplanted to the garden after the danger of frost has passed. There are modern tricks to getting double flowers—with some strains, the double seedlings will appear to be paler green or have a notched leaf. The singles that sneak through, however, will be just as fragrant. Stocks grow best in cooler weather, when night temperatures fall below 60°F, and are skillfully grown in the greenhouse for cutting. The plants grow from one to several feet with one main columnar stem, a far cry from the branching wonders of the past. One plant was recorded in 1822—when the sand, brine, and moon treatment was still practiced—to have measured more than eleven feet in circumference, although the height is not given.

M. bicornis is best sown where it is to grow in small patches throughout the garden. Plants can be transplanted successfully, but in my experience rarely carry as powerful a scent.

 When seeds of *Mirabilis jalapa* first were grown in Europe after their discovery in Peru in the sixteenth century, gardeners raved. It was promptly dubbed as the Marvel-of-Peru, and considering the many wonderful flowers discovered in that land, including alstroemeria, sunflowers, and heliotropes, this was high praise indeed. Gerard was not quite content with this, claiming that *M. jalapa* should be considered instead "Marvell of the World, than of Peru alone."

Why all the fuss over this flower? The plants did perform something that was seemingly miraculous—flowers of completely different colors bloomed on a single plant. Gerard described how, "you shall easily perceive that one is not like another in colour, though you shoulde compare one hundred, which flower one day, and another hundred, which you gathered the next day. . . ." Some of the flowers, moreover, had distinctive stripes, which were highly regarded by our ancestors. These

Mirabilis jalapa
Nyctaginaceae

FOUR O'CLOCK

The flowers of *Mirabilis jalapa*, OPPOSITE, open at different hours, depending on
time zones and weather. Its flowers are seen in a moonlit arrangement, ABOVE.

striped forms are rarely seen today.

Mirabilis is Latin for wonderful; *jalapa*
was given in the mistaken belief that the
drug jalap was obtained from the roots. A
case can also be made that the species
name was taken from Jalapa (Xalapa), a
city in eastern Mexico.

The common name Four o'clock was
not applied until much later. England's
often overcast skies allowed the flowers to
remain open during much of the day.
American colonists, who gardened with
more abundant sunshine, found the
flowers would open reliably at four in the
afternoon. In Victorian times it became an
indispensable feature of elaborate floral
clocks in which the blossoms told the time
of day. The French call it *Belle de Nuit*, or
Night Beauty.

While Four o'clock is considered a tender annual, since Gerard's time the tuberous roots have been dug in the autumn
and stored over winter, just as we treat
dahlias today. Henderson gave instructions
for their lifting and storage more than a
century ago, noting that, "Plants from the
old roots will come into flower much earlier than if grown from seed." Even in
cold climates, however, the tubers are
sometimes winter hardy, especially those
planted near foundations. Those in my garden have survived a dozen frightful winters
during my tenure, and were here long before I arrived.

This plant is a favorite of long-beaked
night moths and children. As children, we
used to pull the flowers off and suck their
thin tubes like a straw for the sweet taste.
The shape of the seeds reminded me then
of tiny grenades. Abundant seedlings ex-
plode regularly near last year's plantings.

Ornamental tobaccos are native to the southern hemisphere of the New World. *Nicotiana tabacum* was cultivated extensively for smoking long before the arrival of European explorers, so its country of origin is unknown, although most botanists suspect Central America. It has historically been grown commercially, and it has been an ornamental feature in gardens as well. Gertrude Jekyll described it nicely, calling it "a rather coarse but handsome thing, six feet high, with pink flowers, useful for filling rather large, empty spaces."

Miss Jekyll admired the entire genus, including *N. sylvestris* and especially *N. alata* (synonym *N. affinis*). She proclaimed it "the best" and she found the fragrance of its flowers enchanting, saying, ". . . when twilight comes the white flowers open and the strong sweet scent, of a luscious, tropical quality, is freely given off." Native to South America, Jasmine Tobacco grows to four feet or more and is a perennial in very warm climates. The plants form a rosette of large basal leaves from which the branched flowering stems grow. The five petals of the tubular flowers flare into a star shape. While the flowers close partially by day, especially in the heat, their evening perfume is worth the wait. The plants, which perform admirably in sun or partial sun, benefit from some pruning later in the summer; this tends to rejuvenate them and induce more flowers. Gardeners often make the mistake, as I have, of cutting back all the plants at once, depriving themselves of several weeks of sweet-scented August evenings.

Nicotiana alata
JASMINE TOBACCO

Nicotiana sylvestris
WOODLAND TOBACCO

Nicotiana tabacum
TOBACCO

The inflorescence of **N.** *sylvestris*, BELOW, complements Cosmos. Jasmine Tobacco, **N.** *alata*, OPPOSITE, is arranged with rudbeckia, dill, and wisteria vine.

Hybridists have developed shorter multicolored varieties that stay open during the day. These are excellent garden plants, though they carry but a trace of the fragrance of their heritage. I have found that by planting these hybrids with *N. alata*, natural hybrids often occur in self-sown offspring the following year. These volunteers share characteristics of the parents, and retain the heirloom fragrance.

N. sylvestris is the scene-stealer of the ornamental tobaccos. Its binomial means "of woods." The Argentine native bears a stately inflorescence of flowers often described as candelabra-like. The flowers cascade from a dense central head. They, too, carry a pleasant evening scent and are attractive throughout the day.

Nicotiana may well be the most mispronounced common plant. Most gardeners associate flowering tobacco with nicotine, and try to pronounce the plant name in a like manner. The plants are named for Jean Nicot, the sixteenth-century French ambassador to Portugal who procured the first seeds from a Dutch merchant returning from a West Indies journey and subsequently introduced them to France. The "t" in Nicot is silent, so *Nicotiana* should sound like Nick-oh-she-anna, with the accent on the second syllable.

Ornamental tobaccos are used to advantage in the garden both as backdrops for roses or rudbeckias or as star performers in their own right. They are closely related to petunias, and grow well, albeit taller, with similar treatment. Miss Jekyll pointed out the merits of ornamental tobacco for indoor arrangements. "When cut in the evening when the bloom is open," she said, "it remains expanded in water in the house and gives off its good evening scent." This advice should be taken to heart, for there is no more pleasant way of drifting off to sleep than with a bouquet of the starry flowers on a bedside table.

Nicotiana Solanaceae

Many gardeners have a special affection for the smaller blue flowers of old-fashioned gardens. Their very names conjure ties to our romantic notions, like Forget-me-not for *Myosotis scorpioides* and Blue-eyed Mary for *Omphalodes verna*. What then to make of a flower called Love-in-a-mist? The bestower of this name could certainly turn a phrase. The pale blue flowers, shrouded by a collar of ferny leaves, are at once charming and mysterious.

Nigella damascena came to English gardens about 1570, supposedly from Damascus, as its Latin name suggests—though it grows wild in southern Europe and north Africa as well. *Nigella* is the diminutive form of *niger*, meaning black, and refers to the seeds. It was not the first of its genus to be grown in England; Nutmeg Flower, *N. sativa*, was grown for its aromatic seeds used in cooking. Gardeners

sometimes confused the two plants. The seeds of Love-in-a-mist were worthless as a flavoring, Parkinson noted, and could not be substituted for those of *N. sativa* "as many ignorant persons use to doe."

London nurseryman Thomas Fairchild thought of it as "rather an odd Plant . . . for the Blossom is of a very pale blue Colour, and is encompass'd with shagged Leaves, as if it was ty'd up in a Bunch of Fewel. . . ." (Spelling was much more creative in 1722, when Fairchild wrote *City Gardiner*, but "Fewel" was probably a misprint—he most likely intended to say Fennel, for Parkinson had called it Fennel Flower.) Fairchild continued, ". . . one would not be without it, for the sake of its strange Appearance." This very appearance attracted equally imaginative folk names. Devil-in-a-bush is a bit fierce for a non-poisonous plant, but it was also called Love-entangle, Love-in-a-puzzle, and Jack-in-prison. The French were not to be outdone, dubbing it *Barbe-bleu*, Bluebeard, and *Cheveux de Venus*, Venus' Hair (for reasons known only to the Gallic mind). Another common name was St. Catherine's-flower, an allusion to the similarities between the saint's wheel and the supposedly spoke-like petals, but it requires a strong faith to imagine this.

Love-in-a-mist became a favorite flower of the cottage gardeners. One of its champions was Gertrude Jekyll, who transformed cottage gardening into an art form and *N. damascena* into a cult flower. The variety 'Miss Jekyll' was named for her and is still grown today. She was matter-of-fact about its merit, stating it "is the result of many years' careful selection, and may be said to be the best garden *Nigella*. The col-our is a pure, soft blue of a quality distinctively its own." There is hardly need for further elaboration.

N. damascena grows to about eighteen inches and normally blooms in midsummer. Many gardeners make sowings in autumn, early spring, and late spring for a succession of bloom throughout the season. Each gardener will discover a rhythm to time the appropriate month for seeding, for Love-in-a-mist is an adaptable plant and grows well in widely diverse situations. I am content in my garden to let *N. damascena* seed itself in carefree fashion, admiring the flowers in July, and later, the handsome striped seedpods.

Nigella damascena
Ranunculaceae

LOVE-IN-A-MIST

The blossoms of *Nigella damascena*, OPPOSITE, are set in a fringe of thread-like foliage; the sky blue variety was named for Gertrude Jekyll, who selected them for color in her garden in Surrey. Self-sown Love-in-a-mist, *N. damascena*, ABOVE, thrives growing in close quarters with grey Artemisia, pink Cranesbill, and Jerusalem Sage at Barnsley House.

Besides being frightened out of my wits when I first saw *The Wizard of Oz* as a child, I was intrigued to learn that poppies could make people—and lions—fall fast asleep. The image of the wicked witch as she hovered over her crystal ball, croaking eerily, "poppies will put them to sleep," is burned in my memory. I associated the poppies with evil and winged monkeys, and I kept a safe distance from my mother's orange poppies when they bloomed each June. I'd never heard of opium, of course, and it was many years later that I found my mistrust for Oriental poppies had been pointless, for the mysterious sleep poppies are *Papaver somniferum*.

The Opium Poppy is one of the oldest cultivated plants; seeds have been found in prehistoric caves, though how one finds something that tiny is beyond me. Throughout history, the flowers and its narcotic by-products have played a large role in many cultures. Legend tells us that when the wheat crop was failing miserably under the care of weary and fretful Ceres, Somnus, the god of sleep, created the poppy to ease her cares and lull her to sleep (some might argue that it was created to exploit Ceres and get more work out of her). After her sleep, she revived and so did the wheat, and that is why Ceres is usually shown with a garland of poppies and corn in her hair, and a stupid smile on her face. Ancient people believed that poppies made wheat grow better (which might also have been used as an excuse for poor weeding).

The original home of the Opium Poppy is not known, though it now has an extensive range throughout the entire Mediterranean region and the Middle East, and is naturalized in many other countries. The Romans probably introduced the flower to England, where it was used widely as a medicinal plant. Gerard warned that, "It mitigateth all kinds of paines, but it leaveth behinde it oftentimes a mischiefe woorse than the disease it selfe. . . ."

The double-flowered varieties, introduced from Constantinople, became popular by the end of the sixteenth century. Clergyman William Hanbury wrote that, "Their doubleness is wonderful . . . their colour no less amazing. . . ." He went on to tell that "Some are so finely variegated, their colours so opposite, and many so delightfully spotted that the finest carnation cannot excel them. . . ." Not surprisingly, *P. somniferum* was called Carnation Poppy or Violet Poppy and Feathered Poppy. Some herbalists mention that the flowers carried an unpleasant scent. Elizabethan ladies came to call it John Silver-pin—"fair without and foul within."

The euphemisms continue to this

O P I U M   P O P P Y

Double forms of *P. somniferum*, OPPOSITE, contrast with singles, TOP. Opium poppies bloom, ABOVE.

day—Lettuce-leaf Poppy is currently in use. Many gardeners are unwilling to admit to growing an illegal plant, and prefer to ignore the flower's illicit past. Ironically, it is quite legal to sell the seeds (they

haven't a trace of the drug in them) and poppy-seed rolls, breads, and cakes everywhere are sprinkled with the seeds of *P. somniferum*.

Opium Poppies were grown as a commercial crop in England in the early nineteenth century. In 1823, Elizabeth Kent related almost casually in *Flora Domestica* that "the solution of opium in spirits of wine is now called laudanum, or loddy, so much used instead of tea by the poorer class of females in Manchester and other manufacturing towns." In other words, they were hooked. In fact, many Victorians took opium, some unwittingly. Patent medicines of the era relied heavily on opium and other drugs. Infamous temperance advocate Carrie Nation, who led the American movement (axe in hand) to prohibit alcohol at the turn of this century, was reputedly addicted to the opium in her patent tonics.

It takes acres of the plants to produce the raw drug from the sap of the seed-head, and Opium Poppies are grown by modern gardeners for their beauty alone. They bloom in early summer on stems growing to three feet or more. The duration of bloom is brief but spectacular. Accordingly, gardeners often plant zinnias or cosmos to fill in the gaps when the poppies are removed. *P. somniferum* thrives in sunny situations without particular attention, and tolerates drought. Because the seedlings resent root disturbance and transplant poorly, gardeners often sow the seed in the autumn or early spring, or allow the plants to seed themselves.

Papaver somniferum Papaveraceae

The longest-lasting legacy of Victorian bedding practices must surely be that of the pelargonium —we're at least a century behind the times to call them Geraniums—and the scarlet rivers of color they cut through park lawns

Nearly all three hundred species of *Pelargonium* are native to southern Africa; they are especially plentiful around the Cape of Good Hope. Among the first species to reach England was *P. peltatum*, the Ivy-leaved Geranium, in 1701. The principal parent of the bedding plants, *P. zonale* (named for the horseshoe markings on the leaves), followed nine years later. By the middle of the century, *Geranium africanum*, as it was then classified, was all the rage.

Yet another group of *Pelargonium* species, the so-called scented geraniums, have inspired a legion of collectors for almost four hundred years. The honor of being the very first *Pelargonium* grown in England belongs to *P. graveolens*, Rose Geranium, coming into cultivation in 1690. Fragrant plants were more valued at that date than at present, and *P. graveolens*—the specific epithet means aromatic—excited gardeners by the uncannily similar scent of its leaves to those of roses. The original species has cleft grey-green leaves on two-foot tall plants with pale moth-like flowers, and, of course, release a lovely smell when the leaves are touched.

A torrent of related species followed. Hybrids and sports of these further swelled the numbers. *P. crispum* smells strongly of lemon. The rigid two-foot stems have uniformly-spaced crinkled

Pelargonium
Geraniaceae

Pelargonium crispum
LEMON-SCENTED GERANIUM

Pelargonium × fragrans
NUTMEG-SCENTED GERANIUM

Pelargonium graveolens
ROSE GERANIUM

Pelargonium tomentosum
PENNYROYAL GERANIUM

Illustration, OPPOSITE, shows the flowers of *P. × fragrans*.
Velvety *P. tomentosum*, LEFT, contrasts with pink Trailing Verbena.
Topiary standards of *P. crispum*, ABOVE, line a greenhouse bench.

leaves; *crispum* means very wavy. One to three flowers of pink with darker stripes bloom at the end of each branch.

Peppermint-scented Geranium, *P. tomentosum*, is distinguished by velvety broad leaves covered with silver hair; *tomentosum* means hairy. The plant is often broader than its common foot in height. Its flowers are white with thin red pinstripes.

The heart-shaped leaves of *P. × fragrans* offered an entirely new scent, that of Nutmeg. One might also say after-shave lotion, but at its date of introduction, 1731, Old Spice was not yet an option. *P. × fragrans*—the name means fragrant, an

original choice—is a shrubby, multi-branched antique hybrid with glaucous foliage and tiny white flowers. It is thought to be descended from the Apple-scented Geranium, *P. odoratissimum*, which suggests nothing of fruit to most noses, but retains the name nonetheless.

Coconut, cucumber, pine, oak, strawberry, apricot—scented species all—were brought into cultivation and, miraculously, survived. The varieties with finely-divided leaves or those with white leaf margins were much admired. In pots and urns, they graced terraces and conservatories. Scented geraniums were purposely placed

near garden gates and doorways so that the long skirts of women might frequently brush the leaves, releasing the pleasant scent. The plants could be brought indoors in winter to relieve musty smells. The leaves became popular in nosegays and in cooking. They could be added to beverages and teas, and Scented Geranium Cake is still a delicacy. The basic recipe is somewhat like that for pineapple-upside-down cake with the leaves substituting for the pineapple at the bottom of the pan. The taste of the resulting cake—the rose-scented leaves are indisputably the best—is indescribably good.

The stiff stems of *P. crispum* are clad with tiny crinkled leaves that smell of lemons, OPPOSITE.
ABOVE, the carmelized leaves of *P. graveolens* can still be seen on a freshly-baked cake.

Hairsplitting botanical differences separate *Perilla* from the genus *Coleus*. In the flower of *Coleus*, but not *Perilla*, the filaments of the stamens are joined from the bases to a height of one-third their length to form sheaths around the styles. The similarities are more obvious. Both exhibit the square stems typical of the mint family, the plants of both are topped by sprays of tiny flowers, and both are grown for their attractive foliage. The flowers of *Perilla* are pale violet.

Perilla frutescens is widely distributed throughout southeastern Asia from India to Japan. Though the plant bears the common name Chinese Basil, it is not to be confused with Sweet Basil, *Ocimum basilicum*, a mint-family relative. *P. frutescens* is a standard culinary herb in Japan (though it has a bitter taste), where it is called *shiso*. Its foliage made the plant a natural for drawing distinct lines in bedding schemes, and it also came to be known as Beefsteak plant in some quarters, although several annuals with dark foliage share this name. It extended the range of conditions where a Coleus-type plant could be used, for *P.*

P. frutescens flowers, ABOVE. Perilla is arranged with *Stachys byzantina, Centranthus ruber,* and pelargoniums, OPPOSITE.

frutescens will thrive in a sunnier location. Shirley Hibberd praised the plant in 1871, asserting, "it cannot be dispensed with, for its solemn bronzy-purple colour gives it a most distinctive character, of great value to the colourist." He cautioned that *P. frutescens* "has been well abused for its 'funereal' aspect, and greatly misused by planters. . . ." Scarcely twenty years later, however, very few gardeners still grew it. Peter Henderson relates that it "at one time was much used as an ornamental border plant, but from its somewhat weedy appearance and wonderful productiveness, it has been pretty generally discarded."

Fashion changes, and what Henderson considered weedy, gardeners today find striking. *P. frutescens* sows itself prolifically if the seed heads are not removed, but the volunteers are readily identifiable the next spring. They transplant easily into beds or borders wherever a substantive foliage is needed. Plantings of summer annuals are enhanced by the addition of Beefsteak Plant. The leaf margins are wavy and deeply toothed. The leaves, with their unusual metallic sheen, are equally dramatic foils for brilliant red Sweet Williams or the pale purple Swan River Daisy, *Brachycome iberidifolia*, as well as Dusty Miller foliage.

Perilla frutescens Labiatae

CHINESE BASIL

Phaseolus coccineus
Leguminosae

SCARLET
RUNNER BEAN

Colonial American vegetable gardens, ABOVE LEFT, bloomed bright with Scarlet Runner Beans. Its brilliant flowers, BELOW LEFT, and its fast-growing vines make *Phaseolus coccineus* a natural for screening wooden fences, ABOVE.

Beans have enjoyed quite a change in fortune since ancient times. Until comparatively recently, the bean was held in low repute. The goddess Ceres excluded the bean from her gifts to mankind, deeming it unworthy. Hippocrates taught abstinence from the bean, lest eating it injure the sight. It was thought beans caused nightmares, or worse, insanity; ghosts fled in a shuddering panic from their smell (one would think this to be an asset, however). Roman priests would not speak the word, thinking it a thing unholy. Certain Egyptians believed that upon leaving their bodies at death, souls became beans; they refused to eat the half-human beans.

In the New World, the Aztecs were industriously cultivating the forerunner of *Phaseolus coccineus*, the Scarlet Runner Bean. By the time Europeans first sailed to the Americas, Scarlet Runners were grown extensively. The plant was first seen in Virginia and the seed sent back to England at the beginning of the seventeenth century. Perhaps Captain John Smith, whose life was saved by Pocahontas, sent the seed to his friend John Tradescant, the English naturalist and gardener to Charles I.

Scarlet Runners were much admired in Europe, and became an important vegetable for the home gardener; although they were not considered to be as tasty as French beans, they were much more reliable producers. In her *Pot-pourri from a Surrey Garden*, Maria Theresa Earle (whose only relation to the American writer Alice Morse Earle was a love of horticulture) covered a lot of territory—literally from soup to nuts. She gave the following advice: "Scarlet Runners are very much better boiled whole, if not too old, only partly drained, and butter added at the last; they should be boiled enough to break up when the butter is stirred in." To avoid confusion, she added, "To be served very hot."

The scientific name is surprisingly straightforward—*Phaseolus* is the Greek word for some unknown type of bean, and *coccineus* means scarlet. Scarlet Runners are one of the few vegetables to be considered as ornamental plants in their own right. Perhaps having had their fill of beans, American colonists favored them for the brilliant flowers. Grown on poles or a trellis, the climber displays showy clusters of bright red blossoms. The Dutch developed a white-flowered variety, but the scarlet form has remained an American favorite.

No special culture is needed for Scarlet Runners, which will quickly cover their supports in a sunny position with ample irrigation. Where no trellis is available, they may be trained (with only slight encouragement) to twine into perennial vines. In an attempt to dress up my Silver Lace Vine, *Polygonum aubertii*, I planted Scarlet Runner seeds at its base. The blooms appeared far earlier than the Silver Lace and lasted the summer, enfolded by a fleece of white flowers in late August.

Ricinus communis
Euphorbiaceae

CASTOR-OIL PLANT

The Castor-oil Plant or Castor Bean is an impressive native of tropical Africa. It was introduced to English horticulture in 1548, but was not grown extensively until the advent of glass houses. The seeds could then be started early and the plants set out for bold displays during the summer. In the nineteenth century, when all things tropical were in vogue, Castor Bean enjoyed prominent positions in formal gardens, especially as a dot plant surrounded by fancy-leaf geraniums.

Ricinus, the Latin name for tick, was used for Castor-oil Plant because the seeds were thought to resemble a European type of the insect. *Communis* means common, and since there is but one species in the genus, it is definitely the common one. In its native habitat, the plants are perennial and can attain twenty feet in height. Castor Beans are naturalized in many tropical countries outside Africa. Varieties with distinctive leaf colors of yellow, red, and grey were selected, some with contrasting veins and deeply-cleft leaves. The common name is derived from the similarity of the oil to castoreum, a strong-smelling oily substance obtained from the sexual glands of the beaver and formerly used in medicines and, of all things, perfumes. The plant is also called *Palma Christi*, Palm of Christ, in South and Central America. This name was also widely used in New England a century ago.

Ricinus became an important commercial as well as ornamental plant. The oil pressed from the seeds has been used for lubricating machinery, and in the production of linoleum, paint, soap, and ink. Many children have wished that its use had been limited strictly to manufacturing, for the oil-rich seeds yields the dreaded Castor Oil, administered as a laxative. Henderson described the vast Castor Bean plantations in Illinois and Missouri where "It is estimated that those States alone produce annually half a million gallons of oil." An acre, by the way, could produce twenty bushels of seeds.

Few plants are as easy to grow, or so gratifying to the gardener's ego. They grow quickly and luxuriantly from seed pressed an inch into the soil, or in areas with cooler or shorter seasons, from greenhouse seedlings. Castor-oil Plant spurts upwards to six feet or more during warm weather with abundant sunshine and water. The flowers are inconspicuous, but they are followed by decorative spiny clusters of seed pods held in the upper half of the plant's interior. The skin of the beans contains the deadly toxin ricin. Where young children are about who have not yet been taught not to eat anything that does not arrive at the dinner table, the flower panicles should be removed before they bear fruit.

R. communis is definitely not a candidate for the tiny courtyard garden, but where a strong foliage statement is needed, this is the plant. The shiny leaves are produced on strong stalks that rarely need staking, though it is advisable to do so in windy areas (any broom handle will do). The leaves have five to eleven toothed lobes, and it is not unusual for them to measure a foot or more across. It is quite acceptable to indulge in Victorian-style opulence, contrasting the show-stopping plants with those of a finer texture, such as *Artemisia*

lactiflora, cosmos, and cleome. The old-fashioned Golden-Glow, *Rudbeckia laciniata* 'Hortensia', is a handsome companion with its eight-foot stems topped with double flowers.

Castor Beans are rarely seen as container plants, but there is much to be said for growing them as such. They impart a lush feeling to a terrace, and life in a pot thwarts their impulse to grow to six feet.

The broad palmate leaves and towering stature of Castor-oil Plant, *Ricinus communis*, OPPOSITE, dwarf clumps of herbs. Clusters of the tiny flowers—nearly hidden by its leaves—ABOVE, are later replaced with spiny seed pods containing spotted beans of a highly poisonous nature. A potted red-veined variety stays at a manageable height, TOP, surrounded by petunias, marigolds, and barrel-grown roses.

Rudbeckia hirta was originally confined to the Great Plains but it is now found in nearly every state. Henderson wrote more than a century ago how in New Jersey it was "becoming common in our meadows, having been introduced by the seed being mixed with the various grass seeds coming from the West, principally from Kentucky." The seeds of the Black-eyed Susan had previously crossed the Atlantic in 1714 and the immigrant was embraced enthusiastically. Some Europeans found the rudbeckias that were rapidly arriving from America—*R. laciniata, R. fulgida*, and those coneflowers now classified as *Echinacea*—too coarse and brassy for their taste. Nonetheless, these very American flowers were widely grown in Europe, although they were largely ignored in their native land.

Fortunes changed for *R. hirta* in the nineteenth century when hybridists began to select more colorful strains. With such an increasingly wide geographic range, it was only natural that hybrids of outstanding character would be developed. Wild Black-eyed Susan was transformed into the garden Gloriosa Daisy. As a wildflower, *R. hirta* is a biennial or short-lived perennial, but Gloriosas bloom prolifically from seed the first year. Not only that, they bloom over a very long period on freely-branched stems, and seem oblivious to hot weather.

The double or single flowers still display the distinctive dark brown central disc surrounded by petals, known as ray-florets, of golden yellow, chestnut red, burnt sienna, or a combination of rustic tones. The

Rudbeckia hirta
Compositae

Gloriosa Daisies, ABOVE, spark
a perennial garden. Red-flushed petals,
RIGHT, distinguish the Gloriosa
Daisy from wild *R. hirta.*

flowers measure three to five inches across,
and are displayed on plants three feet tall.
They are excellent for arranging.

It takes no great horticultural skill to
manage an impressive swath of Gloriosa
Daisies glowing in the border. Plants may
be grown from seed sown *in situ*, or transplanted from an earlier indoor sowing for

them, the golden flowers of the Gloriosas
are accented by lavender and purple liatris,
campanula, and the airy sprays of four-foot
Verbena bonariensis. I call this my "school
colors" border, after a rival crosstown high
school I remember from my youth that
sported gold and purple. The combination
is—well, gaudy, but All-American.

GLORIOSA DAISY

earlier bloom. They need fertile, well-
drained soil in a sunny location. Watering
during dry spells and dead-heading are the
only required tasks. Though they are commonly treated as annuals, the plants often
persist longer and commonly leave seedlings behind over the winter.

Gloriosas are assertively bright, and
there is little point in trying to attempt a
subtle effect. They are grand plants, brilliant in the sunshine, and combine striking-
ly with other vivid red, yellow, and orange
flowers. In the "hot" border where I plant

The genus commemorates a father and
son, both named Olaf Rudbeck, who were
successive professors of botany at the University of Uppsala in Sweden, where Linnaeus was a student. Olaf the Elder
founded the botanical gardens at the university; he was also an accomplished gardener who achieved great success with
foreign plants. Rudbeck was somewhat of
a national celebrity, "for having made the
discovery that the Paradise of Scripture
was situated somewhere in Sweden." Only
the Swedes took any notice of this news.

It is fascinating today to read Alice Morse Earle, for she paints such a lively picture of gardening in turn-of-the-century New York State. It is a charming portrait, but she was also practical and highly opinionated. "Salpiglossis . . . is in its azure tint a lovely flower," she wrote, "though it is a kinsman of the despised Petunia" which she disliked on account of its "sickish odor." She also disliked calceolaria, chrysanthemum, callistephus, portulaca, and was downright nasty about Morning Glory. Still, she liked salpiglossis, at least the azure-tinted ones.

S. sinuata was not yet considered an old-fashioned flower in Miss Earle's time, for it had only been introduced in 1824 from Chile. She was correct in describing it as a relative of petunia; the two are closely related as members of the Nightshade family, although Painted Tongue, as salpiglossis came to be called, is not fragrant. (Early petunias were heavily fragrant, as Miss Earle noted, but wholesale hybridization, for better or worse, has left them with just a faint sweet scent.)

Salpiglossis is from the Greek *salpinx*, a trumpet, and *glossa*, a tongue, alluding to the tongue-like style in the mouth of the corolla. Could botanists have concocted a slurpier muddle of a name? The binomial

Salpiglossis sinuata Solanaceae

PAINTED TONGUE

sinuata means wavy and refers to the leaves. The erect stems and the leaves are covered by glandular hairs which are decidedly clammy to the touch. Plants branch freely

and grow to two or three feet, and the flowers open more than two inches wide.

Painted Tongue blooms in a jewel-box of colors including cream, rose, scarlet, purple, russet, orange, violet blue, and all shades of yellow and gold. Many gardeners steer clear of plants that flower in "mixed" colors, but they may plant *S. sinuata* with a clear conscience. Gertrude Jekyll, who spent more time pondering the nature of color in the garden than most of us have spent gardening, found salpiglossis to be "one of the best late summer annuals, in a series of colourings all of which are very beautiful, and although much varied in tinting, from cream colour through shades of rose and crimson to deepest purple, all go well together." Some flowers are of a single tint, while others feature dark veining like a scalloped spider web; combined with the brilliant hues, these dark overlays are reminiscent of stained glass. Painted Tongue is an elegant late summer bloomer and the patterns of the flowers may be more closely examined in bouquets.

Salpiglossis succeeds best where summers are not excessively warm. The seeds may be sown when the weather has settled and the danger of severe frost is past, or seedlings may be started earlier in a cool greenhouse. Well-drained fertile soil is preferable, as well as a good supply of moisture. A mulch may be beneficial during hot weather to keep the roots cool.

A bouquet, OPPOSITE, combines Painted Tongue, *Salpiglossis sinuata*, with *Campanula carpatica* and *Potentilla thurberi*. The varied blossoms of *Salpiglossis sinuata* are freely produced on branching stems, ABOVE; the "selfs" are one color only, without contrasting throat coloration and with less noticeable veining.

The name *Salvia* stems from the Latin *salvo*, meaning to save, referring to the plant's healing qualities. Many species among the hundreds of *Salvia* found worldwide have been used to treat aching muscles, colds, headaches, inflamed throats, and sores. Clary Sage has been used for many centuries to treat eye complaints. Sage leaves were once rubbed on the gums and teeth for a fresh minty breath and to remove stains. An ancient Arabian proverb asks, "How shall a man die who has sage in his garden?" The answer is that he will go eventually—some graveyards in England were traditionally planted with sage—but he will have better eyesight and whiter teeth in the meantime.

Clary Sage, *S. sclarea*, grows wild in southern Europe and eyewashes have been made from its seeds and leaves since medieval days. *Sclarea* is a corruption of the Latin *clarus*, meaning clear. One traditional treatment called for a whole seed to be placed under the eyelid until it dropped out, for it was thought that several such applications would, according to Nicholas Culpeper, "take off a film which covereth the sight; a handsome and safe remedy, it is a great deal easier than to tear it off with a needle." Mercy!

A kitchen-garden bouquet, OPPOSITE, features Clary Sage, Grape vine, Asparagus fern, Garlic, Verbena, and *Campanula punctata*. Illustration, ABOVE, shows *S. farinacea*. *S. sclarea* blooms impressively, ABOVE RIGHT.

Salvia Labiatae

Salvia argentea   SILVERY CLARY

Salvia elegans   PINEAPPLE SAGE

Salvia farinacea   MEALY-CUP SAGE

Salvia patens   GENTIAN SAGE

Salvia sclarea   CLARY SAGE

Salvia viridis   PURPLE-TOPPED CLARY

The seeds were also beaten to a powder and added to wine as an aphrodisiac. Clary Sage beer was once a celebrated beverage, and the grapefruit smell of the plant recalls that of soda. The smell is not agreeable to everyone; a neighbor once returned a bouquet containing them, saying they smelled like "stinking weeds from Texas."

The plants are biennial, forming rosettes of eight-inch grey-green leaves the first year. These are valuable in the garden even then, for they give the appearance of large hairy hostas. Flowering stalks rise from three to five feet the second year in airy pastel panicles. The small white and lavender flowers are encased by a large mauve bract. Gertrude Jekyll explained her admiration—"the whole effect of the large branching spike of mixed and broken colour being extremely delightful to an eye trained to colour." To the untrained, too.

Purple-topped Clary, *Salvia viridis*, often goes by the name of *S. horminum*, and was grown as early as the sixteenth century in England. It can be found growing in rocky places throughout continental Europe. As with Clary Sage, the bracts of the flowers are important to its distinctive look, in this case more than the tiny flowers they hold. While *viridis* indicates the bracts are green, those of the cultivated forms are extremely colorful. Deep purple, rose, and white varieties are striking. The entire eighteen-inch stem appears to have been hit with a stroke of spray paint, and they fit in gracefully with border plantings where the spring bulbs have gone dormant, as well as in flower arrangements. *S. viridis* grows best in sun and can be sown directly or transplanted.

The new sages introduced during the

first part of the nineteenth century from Mexico attracted a good deal of notice among gardeners for their bright pure colors. Besides the scarlet *S. splendens*, parent of the modern-day bedding hybrids, there were two most noteworthy discoveries. Gentian Sage, *S. patens*, was aptly named for its true blue flowers. The two-foot plants are perennial in their native land, and the tuberous roots can be stored over the winter with the dahlias and gladiolus. Pineapple Sage, *S. elegans*, bears stems of brilliant red blossoms, nearly unparallelled for the intensity of the color, in late summer. (*Lobelia cardinalis* also has a justifiable claim on the title of richest red flower.) The plant emits a delightful fruity scent when the leaves are touched.

ABOVE, *S. viridis* blooms with annuals. *S. patens*, BELOW, grows with nicotiana. OPPOSITE, *S. argentea* nestles in the foreground.

Not every English gardener was so taken with the new sages. The Victorian art critic and writer John Ruskin derided them in 1879 for displaying "no moderation in their hues. The velvety violent blue of the one and scarlet of the other," he fumed, "seem to have no gradation and no shade. There's no colour that gives me such an idea of violence—a sort of rough, angry scream—as that shade of blue, ungradated." It might be argued that Ruskin needed to work out all that hostility. Miss Jekyll, by the way, proclaimed its "pure blue colour" to be "splendid."

Two sages possessing more subtle coloring might have been more to Ruskin's taste. Mealy-cup Sage, *S. farinacea*, came from Texas and New Mexico in 1847. The clusters of small denim-blue flowers are set on a white-dusted stem. The three-foot spikes resemble lavender to a great degree, but regardless of their origin do not stink. Silvery Clary, *S. argentea* (the word means silvery), was introduced from Bulgaria at about the same time. The slender branches of white flowers, though pretty, are not its most impressive feature. The great woolly leaves, up to a foot long, are among the most handsome of all foliage plants. There is hardly a gardener who cannot incorporate more touches of silver into the garden. The rosettes of these great leaves, with furrows and puckers, is "an excellent border plant . . . very showy and ornamental," according to Henderson. The plants are annual, biennial, or—with perfect drainage—perennial, even in cold climes. Silvery Clary is a marvellous addition to large container plantings, where the foliage sets off the other flowers like a huge silver bow.

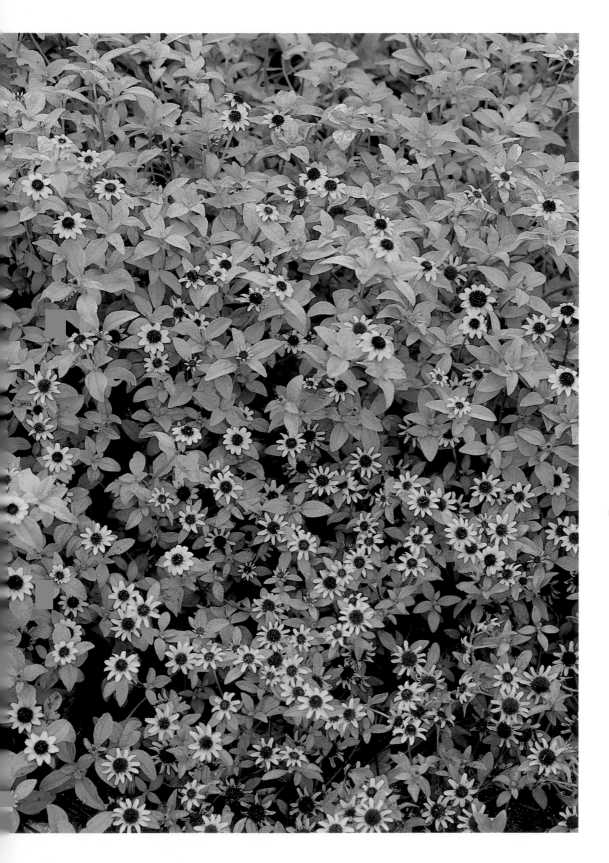

Sanvitalia procumbens was named after professor Federico Sanvitali (1704–1761) of Parma, Italy. It was introduced to English gardens in 1798 from Mexico, and is the only commonly cultivated species of the seven in its genus. The flower is commonly called Creeping Zinnia. Although it is a relative of the Zinnia—both are members of the vast Compositae, the daisy family—the flowers more closely resemble miniature versions of Black-eyed Susan.

Many gardeners have a soft place in their hearts for flowers of this shape and coloration, no matter the size. There is something very appealing about the simple

Sanvitalia procumbens Compositae

CREEPING ZINNIA

A nineteenth-century produce scale, OPPOSITE, weighs *S. procumbens* and plums. Although *S. procumbens* acquired the folk name of Creeping Zinnia, the flowers, LEFT, are distinctly different.

dark-centered discs surrounded by golden rays. The blossoms of sanvitalia are only an inch wide but are borne in great profusion on trailing hairy stems. Each blossom is displayed against a pair of leafy bracts. There is some disagreement about the exact color of the center—is it black, dark brown, or dark purple? In the double form, it disappears entirely. The plants are only six or eight inches high and spread to a foot wide.

S. procumbens had stiff competition for attention upon its introduction. Central and South America proved to be the source of so many outstanding plants during the course of their exploration that sanvitalia took a back seat. Even so, it was not without its admirers; influential gardeners such as Shirley Hibberd and Gertrude Jekyll grew it in their own gardens.

The plant found great favor among early rock gardeners, when scale was not as well considered as it might have been. In today's naturalistic rockeries, the spreading mounds would soon overcome tiny alpine cushions and buns, and the unwanted seedlings would be difficult to extricate from rock crevices.

For gardens of a larger scale that incorporate bigger plants, Creeping Zinnia fits

in beautifully, spilling onto paths and softening embankments. It looks best in vast irregular drifts, which it will form on its own if allowed to do so. Sanvitalia is rarely seen planted in containers, but it will perform admirably in them with tireless bloom. Its trailing habit is best displayed tumbling from the side of a terra-cotta pot of mixed annuals. Entire stems may be cut for bouquets—they will never be missed, and they last for weeks in water.

Excellent effects can be achieved with *S. procumbens* with very little effort. The plants may be sown directly where they are to grow, or transplanted from the greenhouse. Creeping Zinnia has made a comeback in recent years because nurseries are able to offer blooming six-packs in the spring. As might be obvious from its look and place of origin, sanvitalia thrives in heat and sun. It is drought tolerant to a degree, but performs best in well-drained sandy loam with regular irrigation. It fares poorly when it sits with wet feet. There is no maintenance involved, except for thinning the seedlings in the spring to four inches apart. The flowers start to bloom in June and continue until frost without dead-heading, for—like some ovens—they are self-cleaning.

S. procumbens spills into the pathway of a
sunny urban garden, LEFT, with grey
Artemisia and hybrid nicotiana.
S. procumbens, Lobelia, and Marguerite
Daisy bloom in an urn, ABOVE.

When John Tradescant the Elder was appointed Keeper of His Majesty's Garden in 1628, English sea captains and ambassadors throughout the world were alerted that he sought "slipes, seedes, and rootes" of unusual plants. Along with his son, also named John, and through a network of friends and horticultural enthusiasts, Tradescant introduced hundreds of plants to English soil. Among them was *Scabiosa atropurpurea*, which at first was mistakenly called Indian Scabious, although it is a native of southern Europe.

The first seeds produced blossoms of a somber purple tone—*atropurpurea* means deep purple—and so the folk name Mourning Bride was bestowed. It also came to be called Blackamoor's Beauty and Mournful Widow. The French knew it as *Fleur de Veuve*, Widow's-flower, and it was called the same, *Fior della vedova*, in Italy. The morbid theme extended even further: it was woven into funeral wreaths in Portugal. Despite the common name Sweet Scabious, the flowers have little or no scent, although one eighteenth-century description mentions a musky fragrance.

Seeds of other hues arrived, one the color of "redd velvett," and pastel flowers were slowly selected. The colors are varied and soft: lavender, rose, pink, salmon, pale yellow, and white. The original dark shades are among the deepest tones found, and are highly effective in some color schemes. *S. atropurpurea* is also called Pincushion-flower for the protruding stamens clustered in the center, but the allusion is easier seen in the perennial species *S. caucasica*.

Mourning Bride grows to three feet and it is advantageous to pinch young plants to encourage branching. Seeds can be sown outdoors, but in areas with a short growing season, plants are normally started earlier under glass. The seedlings need to be spaced closely together—six to nine inches—to give a full effect, or interplanted among nicotiana or lunaria to avoid a stiff look. The flowers are held on long wiry stems, a boon to flower arrangers. Bees and butterflies visit the flowers, and if they are picked or dead-headed, the flowers will bloom until cut down by frost. Mourning Bride does best in a sunny situation and a mulch helps to cool the roots and keep the soil moist.

"It sounds like a disease," I once heard a woman exclaim at a nursery. No, it was the cure for one. *Scabiosa* is from the Latin *scabies*, to itch; the genus was extensively used by herbalists to treat skin disorders.

Scabiosa atropurpurea
Dipsacaceae

MOURNING BRIDE

The pastel selections of *S. atropurpurea*, OPPOSITE, hardly recall the somber aspects
ascribed to the deep-toned flowers shown in the illustration, TOP.
The blossoms, ABOVE, charmingly complement white Jasmine Tobacco.

Schizanthus was discovered in Chile and introduced to Western horticulture in 1822. The genus is confined to South America, and several closely-related species, notably *S. pinnatus* and *S. retusus*, became the parents of a hybrid group known as *S. × wisetonensis*, named for Wiseton, England, where the first interbreeding was accomplished. That these delicate beauties count potatoes, eggplants, and tomatoes among their kin is surprising.

The name comes from the Greek *schizo*, to divide, and *anthos*, a flower, referring to its deeply divided corolla—the characteristic split lip. Schizanthus is commonly called Butterfly Flower for the spreading multicolored petals resembling wings in flight. The Victorians called them, rather unimaginatively, Fringe-flower.

Though schizanthus was often grown in the grandest conservatory, it could also brighten the humblest window ledge for a penny packet of seed—the Poor Man's Orchid. The cool conditions near the glass in the days before central heating were to its liking, and schizanthus flowers made pretty wintertime decorations on the window ledge with geraniums, Christmas Cactus, and snow falling outside.

The erect branched stems of *Schizanthus*

An understated planting, OPPOSITE, combines *Schizanthus × wisetonensis*, variegated-leaved *P. graveolens*, and a common pelargonium in a vintage terra-cotta pot. A brick terrace, ABOVE, is enriched by the summer display of Poor Man's Orchids.

× wisetonensis display alternate leaves, much divided and distinctly ferny. A profusion of flowers in bunched clusters bloom in shades of pink, rose, coral, peach, white, lavender, violet, and maroon. They are blotched with darker tracings near the center, and the upper lip is streaked with yellow. Height depends strictly on culture. From an early greenhouse sowing in the late autumn, the plants may be potted up to larger sizes throughout the winter before the roots become potbound. Patient gardeners will be rewarded with tubs of specimens, measuring three feet in diameter and bearing thousands of flowers.

Smaller plants from a spring sowing are equally serviceable. Seedlings may be transplanted to the garden after the danger of frost has passed and eventually reach a foot or more. Pinching the growth tips encourages bushiness. The stems are brittle and need protection from wind, or a stake for support. They may be planted in tubs and large pots with stiffer-stemmed plants, like geraniums and Marguerites, which provide a natural and inconspicuous network of support. Care should be taken not to overwater young plants, but as they mature they need frequent applications of water and fertilizer. Poor Man's Orchid thrives in a sunny site with cool temperatures; in mild climates the flowers bedeck patios and terraces during the spring.

Schizanthus × wisetonensis
Solanaceae

POOR MAN'S ORCHID

Strolling through a public garden once, I overheard two women discussing the plants in a bedding display. "What's that?" asked one, to which her friend replied, "Oh, that's Dusty Springfield." While I tried to disguise my laughter as a sudden allergy attack, I tried to understand her comment. Perhaps the name of the silvery-blond singer of the sixties, whose big hit was "You Don't Have to Say You Love Me," as I recall, was much more relevant to her than Dusty Miller. Today our bread is sold in carefully wrapped plastic bags, and we rarely see the baker, much less the flour-covered man who milled the wheat. The name Dusty Miller for *Senecio cineraria* may fade into oblivion.

The Victorians coined the common name, although it has been applied to several other grey-leaved plants. Dusty Miller was a bedding plant *par excellence* in the nineteenth century, though it was first introduced to English gardens about 1750 from southern Europe. Hibberd suggested that the "silver-frosted" leaves were valuable as a contrast with coleus.

This plant has gone through plenty of name changes since then. It was originally *Cineraria maritima*, which meant, roughly, "ash-coloured leaves from the seaside." It was lumped together with the genus *Senecio* (from the Latin *senex*, meaning an old man, referring to the fluffy, white seed heads) as *S. maritimus*, but that, too, was changed. The present form translates basically as "white grey." Many gardeners are surprised to find Dusty Miller shares the same genus with the brilliantly-colored potted daisies from the flower shop, properly *S. × hybridus*, but called cinerarias. Dusty Miller found its way into the genus by virtue of the yellow mop-head flowers that clearly mark it as a member of the daisy tribe. Many gardeners never see these flowers, for grown as an annual, Dusty Miller rarely blooms. The foliage is the thing—downy, finely-lobed leaves that have immense garden value. The plant grows to a foot or so the first year, but often surprises the gardener with a return engagement the following spring. It will then double in size and display the tight clusters of golden-yellow blossoms. It's often been advised to cut them off, but that is rubbish, for they crown the hand-

some leaves with distinction. When, through pure chance, the gardener situates them perfectly, they behave as true perennials, but there is no surefire formula for success, although excellent drainage is a key factor. Despite their Mediterranean origin, about fifteen Dusty Millers have weathered five Colorado winters in my garden.

Dusty Miller is truly an adaptable plant, for aside from its ability to showcase other flowers with its own silver coloration, it grows well in beds, borders, and containers. It is a pretty feature in window boxes combined with trailing lobelias, petunias, and such. I have never seen it recommended for a shady position, but I plant it extravagantly in pots with begonias and impatiens to highlight their jewel-toned flowers. Seedlings come easily from an early spring sowing in the greenhouse or under lights, and the plants are rarely troubled by pests or disease.

Perhaps in fifty years, when planting silvery Dusty Springfield in May, a gardener will wonder how it came to be called by that name. Perhaps too, he will consult his grandmother's obsolete gardening book for the answer.

Senecio cineraria Compositae

DUSTY MILLER

Several plants with grey foliage have been dubbed as Dusty Miller over the years; *Senecio cineraria* holds the most valid claim for the name. Mature plants, RIGHT, bloom with button-like flowers above the silver leaves, enhancing a garden of roses.

Tithonia rotundifolia is native to Mexico and Central America, and was introduced early in the nineteenth century. It was named after Tithonius, the king of Troy, who was loved by Aurora, the goddess of the dawn. She asked Zeus for immortality for her handsome consort, but forgot to include eternal youth in the request. Waking one morning to find her lover-boy had gotten a bit long in the tooth, the superficial Aurora turned him into a grasshopper. What all this has to do with this flower is beyond me.

The binomial *rotundifolia* means round-leaved, though that's not quite true; the leaves look very much like those of sunflowers. In fact, the botanical differences between the species of *Helianthus* and those of *Tithonia* are inconsequential to gardeners—the biggest distinction is that sunflowers are yellow and the Mexican Sunflower is orange. Bright, fiery orange, one might say. The plants grow from four to seven feet, on stout stalks clad with six- to twelve-inch velvety leaves of dark greyed green. The flower stems that originate in the leaf axils are up to a foot long, thickening noticeably underneath the three-inch flower heads.

T. rotundifolia revels in warmth and sunshine. It may be started easily from seed planted in the garden or transplanted from the greenhouse. Well-drained soil and a nitrogen-poor diet serve the plant best, otherwise it will run to leaves and stems at the expense of the blooms. The plants supply long-stemmed flowers for arranging from midsummer to late autumn.

With their impressive stature, Mexican Sunflowers need room to grow and space to be appreciated. I read once that they are not well adapted to small, intimate areas. The warning came too late, for I had planted two in tubs flanking the entrance to a "small, intimate" garden. The containers were three feet high to begin with, and as the pair of tithonia in them leapt to their normal height (I never measured them, lacking a ladder that tall, but I swear they were closer to nine than six feet) the grand effect I had originally envisioned became claustrophobic. Even worse, the up-facing flowers at the tops of those towering stems were enjoyed only by passing aircraft. Thankfully, a violent windstorm toppled the giants in August, putting an end to my shame. Incidentally, some varieties only grow to three feet.

Tithonia rotundifolia
Compositae

MEXICAN SUNFLOWER

Mexican Sunflower thrives in the sun, OPPOSITE, where the flowers shine orange-red. They can easily reach six feet by midsummer, ABOVE, rendering them useful as temporary hedges.

Trachymene coerulea
Umbelliferae

BLUE LACE FLOWER

Trachymene is derived from the Greek *trachys*, rough, and *meninx*, a membrane, referring to the seeds. At one point Blue Lace Flower was segregated as *Didiscus*, under which name gardeners have grown it for one hundred years. The only two species in that genus, however, were reinstated as *Trachymene*. Gardeners have never gotten over it.

Blue Lace Flower was found in Australia and introduced in 1828. As the shape of the flowers suggests, it is a member of the Carrot family. The flower heads are composed of many small individual blossoms. Tiny white stamens rise above the dome of flowers, further adding to the illusion of lace. They resemble those of Queen Anne's Lace, *Daucus carota*, but are characterized by their tint of powder blue. The binomial *coerulea* means, predictably, blue.

The plant has thin stems with a scanty grey-green foliage of thin divided leaves. The branching plants grow to between eighteen and thirty inches, making them suitable candidates for the second tier of a border. With their airy grace, they are well-situated behind shorter, but more substantial companions, including petunias, cranesbills, or ageratums. Blue Lace Flower fits perfectly into a cottage-style garden.

The plants thrive in well-drained sandy loam in full sun, blooming in July and August. Planting them in clay soil will not produce good results. They may be sown directly in the spring or transplanted, though every precaution should be taken not to disturb the roots. Some gardeners use degradable peat pots for this purpose.

A mulch will keep the roots cool, for the plants are sensitive to extreme heat.

Because of the soft tint of its flowers, Blue Lace Flower has long been a florist's favorite. The flowers are evocative of charming bouquets from bygone days, and are especially pretty with pastel roses. By

Blue Lace Flower, OPPOSITE, is among but a handful of Australian annuals that found favor in England and America. Freshly-cut Blue Lace Flowers, inserted in florist's water picks, ABOVE, enliven a bouquet of dried everlastings.

inserting the stems into what are called "picks"—water-filled tubes with a rubber cap that snugly accommodate a single stem—the flowers may be added to dried arrangements. The effect of Blue Lace is especially pleasing against the amber tones and texture of the dried flowers.

Tropaeolum majus is a most curious-looking plant. Were it not so common, and gardeners not so accustomed to the lily-pad leaves borne on squiggly stems adorned by spurred flowers, it might elicit more excitement. Imagine the response in the late sixteenth century when explorers from the expanding Spanish empire first sent seed from Peru to botanists in Europe. The plant astounded them, as well it might. (As a child I imagined Nasturtium, for some reason, to be from the moon.) Dr. Nicholas Monardes, whose speciality and passion was exotic flowers from the New World, was enthralled, and he requested more seed and information from travellers and missionaries. He called it Blood Flower, as the first specimens he grew must have been red. Gerard had received the seed by 1597 from the keeper of the King's Garden in Paris.

Linnaeus thought the leaves resembled a shield, and the flowers spear-pierced, bloodstained helmets. What an imagination the "Father of Botany" had. He consequently named the genus *Tropaeolum*, from the Greek *tropaeum*, a pillar erected on the battlefield to display the armor of vanquished foes. Linnaeus' daughter, Elizabeth, reported that during a still evening she could discern eerie electric rays emanating from nasturtiums in the garden. Modern botanists have not been able to verify this phenomenon; the entire household may have been highly imaginative.

The English called the plants Indian Cress or Nasturtium, for they had a spicy taste. Nasturtium is derived from the Latin

Tropaeolum
Tropaeolaceae

Tropaeolum majus NASTURTIUM

Tropaeolum peregrinum CANARY CREEPER

Tropaeolum speciosum
SCOTCH FLAME-FLOWER

nasus tortus, distorted nose, because of the plant's pungent scent. To confuse matters, there is a valid genus named *Nasturtium*, of which water cress is a member. It is interesting that the common name Nasturtium is not only of classical origin, but rightfully belongs to another plant. The only other example of this I can recall is the case of *Pelargonium* versus *Geranium*—still pending before the Supreme Court—where the common bedding plants are properly *Pelargonium*, though they go by the borrowed common name assigned to the hardy cranesbills. Incidentally, tropaeolums were for many years assigned to the natural order of Geraniaceae, which would have made them either Peruvian pelargoniums or South American geraniums.

Our ancestors considered Nasturtium an edible as well as ornamental plant. The leaves and flowers were eaten in salads and the seeds were ground for a much-prized mustard. An old recipe tells "to pickle the Nerstusan Seeds and Flowers gather the buds whilst they are greene, with the stalks an inch long." The seed is high in Vitamin C; pickled, it's a unique substitute for capers.

T. majus is a trailer or reluctant climber. Samuel Gilbert advised in 1695 how the plants could be trained to grow "on craggy poles . . . to lead up their wiery Branches, which guided by your hand to the top, make a glorious Show." Double-flowered forms were raised in Italy during the eighteenth century, but as they needed to be propagated by cuttings, have largely become extinct.

Hybridizing produced dwarf forms in the nineteenth century that were widely called Tom Thumbs. Seed catalogues from the last century extolled the virtues of new colors—including several on one plant—and other improvements each year.

At this height of their popularity, about 1875, Shirley Hibberd considered Nasturtiums "overrated." While he admired some of the older varieties, he stated bluntly, "Two-thirds, at least, of the newest varieties are worthless." The Tom Thumbs, in particular, he recommended be "consigned to the rubbish heap."

Other species of *Tropaeolum* enjoyed popularity. Canary Creeper, *T. peregrinum*, was discovered by a French naturalist near Lima, Peru, and introduced to European botanists in 1755. The shape of the clustered yellow flowers on the climbing stems suggests birds in flight. The Spanish christened it *Paxarito*, Little-bird-plant. Scotch Flame-flower, *T. speciosum*, was introduced in 1847 by the famed Veitch Nursery. A wildflower native to Chile, the climber proved hardy in many parts of the British Isles, and thrived in the cool, moist air of Scotland. It is often seen draped on a clipped hedge, where—in the words of one observer in 1882—its sheet of flowers look like "a mass of the scarlet cloth from which soldier's jackets are made." Humphrey John shared in *The Skeptical Gardener* his secret to growing *T. speciosum* outside of Scotland. In his English garden on the eastern edge of the Cotswolds, he grew it "as easily as bindweed." "The recipe is simple," he wrote, "get half a bushel of roots from someone who can grow it, plant them in every kind of soil you can compound, and forget all about them. They will thrive ineradicably in several places where you can be sure you would have never planted them. . . ."

Illustration, OPPOSITE, shows Canary Creeper. Nasturtium, OPPOSITE, climbs gracefully. Its leaves and flowers, ABOVE, give salads a spicy taste. *T. speciosum*, BELOW, cloaks a hedge.

Verbena Verbenaceae

Verbena bonariensis TALL VERBENA

Verbena × hybrida ROSE VERVAIN

Verbena rigida LILAC VERBENA

Verbena was a sacred plant to ancient peoples. Romans swept the altar of Jupiter with its branches and it was a part of Persian sun-worshipping ceremonies.

The common name Vervain comes from the old Celtic *ferfaen*—witches' herb—although it was commonly used for protection against witchcraft. "Vervain and dill," said the old rhyme, "hinder witches of their will." Vervain held secret powers to the Druids. It was often employed medicinally as a cure for a variety of ailments. One remedy directed that Vervain roots be tied around the patient's neck with a yard of white satin ribbon until he recovered—and should he not, the corpse was at least gaily festooned for the wake.

Verbena may be a corruption of *Herbena* or *herba bona*, the good herb, "so much in use among the Heathens," according to seventeenth-century French botanist J. Pitton de Tournefort.

The first New World Vervain to reach England was *V. bonariensis* in 1726. The binomial designates it as a plant from Buenos Aires, where it was discovered. It is so different from the bedding plants we call *Verbena* that most gardeners would have trouble putting them into the same genus. Branches grow to four feet with pairs of narrow, pointed leaves. Tiny pale purple flowers are held in dense clusters.

A close relative is Lilac Vervain, *V. rigida* (synonym *V. venosa*), also a native of Argentina and southern Brazil. It was discovered in 1830, also just a stone's throw from Buenos Aires, which must have been remarkably free from witches. It resembles

Tall Verbena but is shorter, growing to two feet or less. When thriving in full sun, the plants are stiffly branched—*rigida* means rigid. A writer in the *Cottage Garden* in 1850 recommended *V. rigida* be combined with scarlet geraniums to give what park-keepers then called the "shot silk effect." Henderson had similar ideas, saying, "Its lilac or bluish flowers are produced in great profusion rendering it a first-rate subject for bedding, especially with silver-leaved Geraniums." He recommended that the roots be stored over winter, from which

V. bonariensis, OPPOSITE, floats above *Sanvitalia procumbens*. The illustration and country bouquet, ABOVE, feature the flowers. *V. rigida*, BELOW, is shorter.

"any number of plants may be propagated in the spring from the young shoots. . . ."

Other species, the parents of the race of Rose Vervains that were to find a prominent place in every Victorian parterre, began to arrive from South America in 1826. At least three species figure prominently in the breeding lines, but the hybridists were extremely poor at documenting the experiments. The results were spectacular, however, and by the 1880s about one hundred named varieties were sold. Hibberd said that of all the bedding annuals, there was not one "that more perfectly answers to the requirements of the garden colourist" than the hybrid *Verbena*. The flat umbels of tightly-packed flowers, some with contrasting center "eyes," provided brilliant pure shades of purple, red, pink, crimson, puce, peach, and white.

Hibberd had to admit that even during his day, however, their popularity was on the wane. He blamed poor culture, claiming the plants were often set out in poor soil and watered insufficiently. The most "grievous mistake," he said, was to strike the cuttings too early in the greenhouse, resulting in poor stock "starving in small pots." The hybrids suffered from spider mites, thrips, and mildew, and were dusted continually with sulphuric powders and other mixtures of poisons that ruined their appearance. The strongest varieties that survived the era were the forerunners of modern *Verbena* × *hybrida*, which closely resembles its Victorian ancestors but has a stronger constitution. Modern gardeners, it should be noted, are generally better horticulturists than the Victorians, most of whom talked a good show but were dismal at plant care.

Zinnia commemorates Johann Gottfried Zinn (1727–1759), a German professor of botany and physics. It was a comparatively late arrival from Mexico; the first species did not appear in England until the eighteenth century. Zinnias had been grown in the gardens of Montezuma, along with dahlias, sunflowers, and morning glories. When the Spanish first invaded the Aztec empire the gardens of the ruler were said to surpass anything in Europe. The horticultural tradition was quite different, too—when planting a new species obtained from far away, Montezuma's gardeners were instructed to prick their ears and sprinkle the plant with the blood. (Most of us perform a somewhat similar ceremony only when pruning roses.)

The Aztecs grew *Zinnia angustifolia*, the so-called Classic Zinnia. The unrecorded history of its cultivation in America may stretch back thousands of years, so it can be honestly called a true classic. The specific epithet *angustifolia* means narrow-leaved, and the plant is quite dissimilar to the image most gardeners hold of Zinnias.

Spreading mounds, up to a foot high, of thin olive-green leaves are covered with single flowers. The blossoms are riveting, for the golden central disc is surrounded by ray-florets of intense coloration. These gamboge-yellow petals are flushed with orange on the margins, and the gradation of tone is nearly fluorescent. Had they been introduced only in the last decade, we might well have called them Disco Daisies.

This may sound a tad gaudy, but the garden worthiness of Classic Zinnia far ex-

ceeds the description. The dark leaves underscore the brightness of the flowers that measure two or less inches across. The flowers may be combined with those of golden tickseed, *Coreopsis lanceolata*, brilliant orange *Geum quellyon*, lavender oregano, *Origanum vulgare*, and Purple-topped Clary,

Salvia viridis, to create a richly colored planting. Like all Zinnias, *Z. angustifolia* is a plant that relishes the summer.

Z. elegans means elegant, although its stature has certainly come up in the world from the time the Indians of Mexico called it Eyesore. The original wild version is a dull lavender color. It was up to nineteenth-century European plantsmen to perform some Cinderella magic on the flower. Work commenced at the time of its introduction in 1829; the first double forms were raised in 1856 in France. In less than a decade a race of colorful hybrids displayed the prim elegance of French millinery. Further breeding during this century has produced tiny dwarves and brazen mammoths, if this is the sort of development one calls progress.

The flowers do not drop their petals as many members of the Compositae family do. That the flowers remain perfect for so long has given the plant one of its common names, Youth-and-old-age. This is the Dorian Gray of the floral world, though it was hybridists, not the devil, who were responsible for its pristine longevity.

Z. haageana may have played a role in the transformation of *Z. elegans*. This species is showier to begin with, sporting scarlet, yellow, or two-toned blooms. It has been improved only slightly over its wild look, although careful selection by Aztec gardeners may have produced better blooms. The flowers measure two inches across, and are produced prolifically on bushy two-foot plants. The old-fashioned 'Old Mexico' and 'Persian Carpet' varieties, still available from seed houses, are very similar to those grown during the nineteenth century.

An antique pot, OPPOSITE ABOVE, displays
Z. angustifolia with perilla, white balsam, and
alliums. The 'Old Mexico' strain of
Z. haageana, OPPOSITE BELOW, is still
grown. ABOVE, Classic Zinnia varies little
from the days of the Aztecs, but *Z. elegans*
owes its size to hybridizers.

Zinnia Compositae

Zinnia angustifolia CLASSIC ZINNIA

Zinnia elegans YOUTH-AND-OLD-AGE

Zinnia haageana MEXICAN ZINNIA

SOURCES

Alcea rosea

ABUNDANT LIFE SEED FOUNDATION; ALBERTA NURSERIES AND SEEDS: FRAGRANT PATH; GRIANÁN GARDEN; HEIRLOOM GARDENS; PARK SEED; RICHTERS; ROCKY MOUNTAIN SEED; SEEDS BLÜM; SELECT SEEDS; SHEPHERD'S GARDEN SEEDS; THOMPSON & MORGAN; W. ATLEE BURPEE.

Amaranthus caudatus

ABUNDANT LIFE SEED FOUNDATION; FRAGRANT PATH; HEIRLOOM GARDENS; RICHTERS; SEEDS BLÜM; SELECT SEEDS; THOMPSON & MORGAN.

Amaranthus tricolor

COOK'S GARDEN; HARRIS SEEDS; PLANTS OF THE SOUTHWEST; SEEDS BLÜM; STOKES SEEDS; THOMPSON & MORGAN; W. ATLEE BURPEE.

Borago officinalis

COMPANION PLANTS; COOK'S GARDEN; FRAGRANT PATH; HEIRLOOM GARDENS; PLANTS OF THE SOUTHWEST; RICHTERS; SEEDS BLÜM; SHEPHERD'S GARDEN SEEDS; SOUTHERN EXPOSURE SEED EXCHANGE; STOKES SEEDS; W. ATLEE BURPEE.

Callistephus chinensis

ABUNDANT LIFE SEED FOUNDATION; ALBERTA NURSERIES AND SEEDS; HARRIS SEEDS; HEIRLOOM GARDENS; PLANTS OF THE SOUTHWEST; ROCKY MOUNTAIN SEED; SHEPHERD'S GARDEN SEEDS; STOKES SEEDS; THOMPSON & MORGAN; VERMONT BEAN SEED CO.; W. ATLEE BURPEE.

Cleome hassleriana

PLANTS OF THE SOUTHWEST; SEEDS BLÜM; SOUTHERN EXPOSURE SEED EXCHANGE; STOKES SEEDS; THOMPSON & MORGAN; VERMONT BEAN SEED CO.; W. ATLEE BURPEE.

WHERE TO FIND THE FLOWERS

The addresses for the nurseries noted below are listed alphabetically beginning on page 150.

Coleus blumei

COLOR FARM GROWERS; HARRIS SEEDS; PLANTS OF THE SOUTHWEST; ROCKY MOUNTAIN SEED; STOKES SEEDS; THOMPSON & MORGAN; VERMONT BEAN SEED CO.; W. ATLEE BURPEE.

Consolida ambigua

ABUNDANT LIFE SEED FOUNDATION; FRAGRANT PATH; GRIANÁN GARDEN; PLANTS OF THE SOUTHWEST; SEEDS BLÜM; SELECT SEEDS; SOUTHERN EXPOSURE SEED EXCHANGE; STOKES SEEDS; W. ATLEE BURPEE.

Consolida orientalis

HARRIS SEEDS; PARK SEED; RICHTERS; ROCKY MOUNTAIN SEED; SHEPHERD'S GARDEN SEEDS; PLANTS OF THE SOUTHWEST; PARK SEED; SHEPHERD'S GARDEN SEEDS; STOKES SEEDS; VERMONT BEAN SEED CO.

Cosmos bipinnatus

ABUNDANT LIFE SEED FOUNDATION; ALBERTA NURSERIES AND SEEDS; FRAGRANT PATH;

Grianán Garden, Park Seed; Plants of the

GRIANÁN GARDEN, PARK SEED; PLANTS OF THE SOUTHWEST; SHEPHERD'S GARDEN SEEDS; STOKES SEEDS; THOMPSON & MORGAN; W. ATLEE BURPEE.

Dianthus barbatus

ABUNDANT LIFE SEED FOUNDATION; ALBERTA NURSERIES AND SEEDS; FRAGRANT PATH; HEIRLOOM GARDENS; PLANTS OF THE SOUTHWEST; RICHTERS; ROCKY MOUNTAIN SEED; SEEDS BLÜM; SELECT SEEDS; THOMPSON & MORGAN; VERMONT BEAN SEED CO.; W. ATLEE BURPEE.

Digitalis purpurea

ABUNDANT LIFE SEED FOUNDATION; ALBERTA NURSERIES AND SEEDS; COMPANION PLANTS; FRAGRANT PATH; GRIANÁN GARDEN; PLANTS OF THE SOUTHWEST; RICHTERS; ROCKY MOUNTAIN SEED; SELECT SEEDS; SHEPHERD'S GARDEN SEEDS; THOMPSON & MORGAN; VERMONT BEAN SEED CO.

Dolichos lablab

FRAGRANT PATH; THOMPSON & MORGAN.

Fuchsia × hybrida

ANNABELLE'S FUCHSIA GARDENS; LOGEE'S GREENHOUSES; MERRY GARDENS; THOMPSON & MORGAN.

Gomphrena globosa

ALBERTA NURSERIES AND SEEDS; FRAGRANT PATH; PLANTS OF THE SOUTHWEST; RICHTERS; SEEDS BLÜM; SHEPHERD'S GARDEN SEEDS; SOUTHERN EXPOSURE SEED EXCHANGE; STOKES SEEDS; THOMPSON & MORGAN; VERMONT BEAN SEED CO.; W. ATLEE BURPEE.

Helianthus annuus

FRAGRANT PATH; GRIANÁN GARDEN; HARRIS SEEDS; HEIRLOOM GARDENS; NATIVE SEEDS;

PLANTS OF THE SOUTHWEST; PARK SEED; RICHTERS; SEEDS BLÜM; SOUTHERN EXPOSURE SEED EXCHANGE; STOKES SEEDS; THOMPSON & MORGAN; VERMONT BEAN SEED CO.; W. ATLEE BURPEE.

Heliotropium arborescens

FRAGRANT PATH; GRIANÁN GARDEN; HARRIS SEEDS; RICHTERS; STOKES SEEDS; THOMPSON & MORGAN; W. ATLEE BURPEE.

Impatiens balsamina

ABUNDANT LIFE SEED FOUNDATION; ALBERTA NURSERIES AND SEEDS; FRAGRANT PATH; HEIRLOOM GARDENS; PLANTS OF THE SOUTHWEST; RICHTERS; ROCKY MOUNTAIN SEED; THOMPSON & MORGAN; VERMONT BEAN SEED CO.

Lathyrus odoratus

ALBERTA NURSERIES AND SEEDS; FRAGRANT PATH;

HARRIS SEEDS; HEIRLOOM GARDENS; PARK SEED; SEEDS BLÜM; SELECT SEEDS; SHEPHERD'S GARDEN SEEDS; STOKES SEEDS; THOMPSON & MORGAN; VERMONT BEAN SEED CO.

Lavatera trimestris

ALBERTA NURSERIES AND SEEDS; FRAGRANT PATH; GRIANÁN GARDEN; PLANTS OF THE SOUTHWEST; SHEPHERD'S GARDEN SEEDS; THOMPSON & MORGAN; W. ATLEE BURPEE.

Malva sylvestris

THOMPSON & MORGAN.

Matthiola bicornis

ALBERTA NURSERIES AND SEEDS; FRAGRANT PATH:
HEIRLOOM GARDENS; PLANTS OF THE
SOUTHWEST; SEEDS BLÜM; THOMPSON &
MORGAN.

Matthiola incana

ABUNDANT LIFE SEED FOUNDATION; ALBERTA
NURSERIES AND SEEDS; FRAGRANT PATH; HARRIS
SEEDS; HEIRLOOM GARDENS; PLANTS OF THE
SOUTHWEST; ROCKY MOUNTAIN SEED; SEEDS
BLÜM; SELECT SEEDS; SHEPHERD'S GARDEN
SEEDS; STOKES SEEDS; THOMPSON & MORGAN;
VERMONT BEAN SEED CO.; W. ATLEE BURPEE.

Mirabilis jalapa

ABUNDANT LIFE SEED FOUNDATION; ALBERTA
NURSERIES AND SEEDS; FRAGRANT PATH; HARRIS
SEEDS; HEIRLOOM GARDENS; PLANTS OF THE
SOUTHWEST; SELECT SEEDS; SOUTHERN
EXPOSURE SEED EXCHANGE; STOKES SEEDS;
THOMPSON & MORGAN; VERMONT BEAN SEED
CO.; W. ATLEE BURPEE.

Nicotiana alata

ABUNDANT LIFE SEED FOUNDATION; FRAGRANT
PATH; GRIANÁN GARDEN; HEIRLOOM GARDENS;
PLANTS OF THE SOUTHWEST; SEEDS BLÜM;
SELECT SEEDS; SHEPHERD'S GARDEN SEEDS;
SOUTHERN EXPOSURE SEED EXCHANGE; STOKES
SEEDS; THOMPSON & MORGAN.

Nicotiana sylvestris

FRAGRANT PATH; PLANTS OF THE SOUTHWEST;
THOMPSON & MORGAN; VERMONT BEAN SEED
CO.

Nicotiana tabacum

COMPANION PLANTS; HEIRLOOM GARDENS;
RICHTERS; THOMPSON & MORGAN.

Nigella damascena

ABUNDANT LIFE SEED FOUNDATION; ALBERTA
NURSERIES AND SEEDS; FRAGRANT PATH;
GRIANÁN GARDEN; HEIRLOOM GARDENS; PLANTS
OF THE SOUTHWEST; RICHTERS; SEEDS BLÜM;
SHEPHERD'S GARDEN SEEDS; STOKES SEEDS;
THOMPSON & MORGAN; W. ATLEE BURPEE.

Papaver somniferum

THOMPSON & MORGAN; VERMONT BEAN SEED
CO.

Pelargonium crispum

COMPANION PLANTS; LOGEE'S GREENHOUSES;
RICHTERS; SHADY HILL GARDENS.

Pelargonium × fragrans

COMPANION PLANTS; LOGEE'S GREENHOUSES;
RICHTERS; SHADY HILL GARDENS.

Pelargonium graveolens

COMPANION PLANTS; LOGEE'S GREENHOUSES;
RICHTERS; SHADY HILL GARDENS.

Pelargonium tomentosum

COMPANION PLANTS; LOGEE'S GREENHOUSES;
RICHTERS; SHADY HILL GARDENS.

Perilla frutescens

COMPANION PLANTS; FRAGRANT PATH; HEIRLOOM
GARDENS; PLANTS OF THE SOUTHWEST;
RICHTERS; SEEDS BLÜM; SOUTHERN EXPOSURE
SEED EXCHANGE.

Phaseolus coccineus

ABUNDANT LIFE SEED FOUNDATION; FRAGRANT
PATH; NATIVE SEEDS; PARK SEED; ROCKY
MOUNTAIN SEED; SEEDS BLÜM; SHEPHERD'S
GARDEN SEEDS; SOUTHERN EXPOSURE SEED
EXCHANGE; W. ATLEE BURPEE.

Ricinus communis

COMPANION PLANTS; RICHTERS; SEEDS BLÜM;
STOKES SEEDS; THOMPSON & MORGAN.

Rudbeckia hirta

ALBERTA NURSERIES AND SEEDS; HARRIS SEEDS;
PLANTS OF THE SOUTHWEST; SEEDS BLÜM;
STOKES SEEDS; THOMPSON & MORGAN;
VERMONT BEAN SEED CO.; W. ATLEE BURPEE.

Salpiglossis sinuata

ALBERTA NURSERIES AND SEEDS; GRIANÁN
GARDEN; HARRIS SEEDS; HEIRLOOM GARDENS;
PLANTS OF THE SOUTHWEST; ROCKY MOUNTAIN
SEED; SEEDS BLÜM; SELECT SEEDS; STOKES SEEDS;
THOMPSON & MORGAN; W. ATLEE BURPEE.

Salvia argentea

COMPANION PLANTS

Salvia elegans

COMPANION PLANTS; RICHTERS; W. ATLEE
BURPEE.

Salvia farinacea

COMPANION PLANTS; GRIANÁN GARDEN; HARRIS SEEDS; PLANTS OF THE SOUTHWEST; STOKES SEEDS; THOMPSON & MORGAN; VERMONT BEAN SEED CO.; W. ATLEE BURPEE.

Salvia patens

THOMPSON & MORGAN; W. ATLEE BURPEE.

Salvia sclarea

COMPANION PLANTS; HEIRLOOM GARDENS; RICHTERS; SEEDS BLÜM; THOMPSON & MORGAN.

Salvia viridis

COMPANION PLANTS; COOK'S GARDEN; RICHTERS; STOKES SEEDS; THOMPSON & MORGAN; W. ATLEE BURPEE.

Sanvitalia procumbens

HARRIS SEEDS; STOKES SEEDS; THOMPSON & MORGAN; VERMONT BEAN SEED CO.

Scabiosa atropurpurea

ABUNDANT LIFE SEED FOUNDATION; ALBERTA NURSERIES AND SEEDS; FRAGRANT PATH; HARRIS SEEDS; HEIRLOOM GARDENS; PLANTS OF THE SOUTHWEST; ROCKY MOUNTAIN SEED; SEEDS BLÜM; SELECT SEEDS; STOKES SEEDS; THOMPSON & MORGAN; VERMONT BEAN SEED CO.; W. ATLEE BURPEE.

Schizanthus × wisetonensis

ALBERTA NURSERIES AND SEEDS; GRIANÁN GARDEN; PLANTS OF THE SOUTHWEST; SEEDS BLÜM; THOMPSON & MORGAN; W. ATLEE BURPEE.

Senecio cineraria

ABUNDANT LIFE SEED FOUNDATION; ALBERTA NURSERIES AND SEEDS; GRIANÁN GARDEN; HARRIS SEEDS; PLANTS OF THE SOUTHWEST; RICHTERS; SEEDS BLÜM; STOKES SEEDS; THOMPSON & MORGAN; W. ATLEE BURPEE.

Tithonia rotundifolia

ABUNDANT LIFE SEED FOUNDATION; HARRIS SEEDS; PLANTS OF THE SOUTHWEST; SEEDS BLÜM; SOUTHERN EXPOSURE SEED EXCHANGE; STOKES SEEDS; THOMPSON & MORGAN; W. ATLEE BURPEE.

Trachymene coerulea

ALBERTA NURSERIES AND SEEDS; FRAGRANT PATH; GRIANÁN GARDEN; PLANTS OF THE SOUTHWEST; THOMPSON & MORGAN; W. ATLEE BURPEE.

Tropaeolum majus

ABUNDANT LIFE SEED FOUNDATION; ALBERTA NURSERIES AND SEEDS; COOK'S GARDEN; FRAGRANT PATH; GRIANÁN GARDEN; HARRIS SEEDS; HEIRLOOM GARDENS; PLANTS OF THE SOUTHWEST; SEEDS BLÜM; SELECT SEEDS; STOKES SEEDS; THOMPSON & MORGAN; VERMONT BEAN SEED CO.; W. ATLEE BURPEE.

Tropaeolum peregrinum

ALBERTA NURSERIES AND SEEDS; COOK'S GARDEN; FRAGRANT PATH; GRIANÁN GARDEN; HEIRLOOM GARDENS; PLANTS OF THE SOUTHWEST; THOMPSON & MORGAN; W. ATLEE BURPEE.

Tropaeolum speciosum

THOMPSON & MORGAN.

Verbena bonariensis

PLANTS OF THE SOUTHWEST; THOMPSON & MORGAN.

Verbena × hybrida

ALBERTA NURSERIES AND SEEDS; HEIRLOOM GARDENS; ROCKY MOUNTAIN SEEDS; STOKES SEEDS; THOMPSON & MORGAN; W. ATLEE BURPEE.

Verbena rigida

COMPANION PLANTS; PLANTS OF THE SOUTHWEST; THOMPSON & MORGAN.

Zinnia angustifolia

PLANTS OF THE SOUTHWEST; THOMPSON & MORGAN; W. ATLEE BURPEE.

Zinnia elegans

HARRIS SEEDS; HEIRLOOM GARDENS; RICHTERS; ROCKY MOUNTAIN SEED; SEEDS BLÜM; SOUTHERN EXPOSURE SEED EXCHANGE; STOKES SEEDS; THOMPSON & MORGAN; W. ATLEE BURPEE.

Zinnia haageana

ALBERTA NURSERIES AND SEEDS; HEIRLOOM GARDENS; SEEDS BLÜM; SOUTHERN EXPOSURE SEED EXCHANGE; STOKES SEEDS; THOMPSON & MORGAN; W. ATLEE BURPEE.

SEED MERCHANTS

The following select list does not represent every seed company that offers antique annuals, but it does include a geographically diverse representation of commercial sources for seeds and some plants in the United States and Canada.

ABUNDANT LIFE SEED FOUNDATION
P.O. Box 772
Port Townsend, WA 98368

ALBERTA NURSERIES AND SEEDS LTD.
Box 20, Bowden
Alberta, Canada T0M 0K0

ANNABELLE'S FUCHSIA GARDENS
32531 Rhoda Lane
Fort Bragg, CA 95437

W. ATLEE BURPEE & CO.
Warminster, PA 18974

COLOR FARM GROWERS
2710 Thornhill Road
Auburndale, FL 33823

COMPANION PLANTS
7247 North Coolville Ridge Road
Athens, OH 45701

THE COOK'S GARDEN
P.O. Box 65
Londonderry, VT 05148

THE FRAGRANT PATH
P.O. Box 328
Fort Calhoun, NE 68023

GRIANÁN GARDEN
P.O. Box 14492
San Francisco, CA 94114

HARRIS SEEDS
60 Saginaw Drive
P.O. Box 22960
Rochester, NY 14692-2960

HEIRLOOM GARDENS
P.O. Box 138
Guerneville, CA 95446

LOGEE'S GREENHOUSES
141 North Street
Danielson, CT 06790

MERRY GARDENS
P.O. Box 595
Camden, ME 04843

NATIVE SEEDS/SEARCH
2509 N. Campbell Avenue, #325
Tucson, AZ 85719

PLANTS OF THE SOUTHWEST
930 Baca Street
Santa Fe, NM 87501

PARK SEED CO.
Cokebury Road
Greenwood, SC 29647-0001

RICHTERS
Goodwood
Ontario, Canada L0C IA0

THE ROCKY MOUNTAIN SEED COMPANY
P.O. Box 5204
Denver, CO 80217

SEEDS BLÜM
Idaho City Stage
Boise, ID 83706

SELECT SEEDS
81 Stickney Hill Road
Union, CT 06076

SHADY HILL GARDENS
821 Walnut Street
Batavia, IL 60510

SHEPHERD'S GARDEN SEEDS
30 Irene Street
Torrington, CT 06790

SOUTHERN EXPOSURE SEED EXCHANGE
P.O. Box 158
North Garden, VA 22959

STOKES SEEDS INC.
Box 548
Buffalo, NY 14240

THOMPSON & MORGAN, INC.
P.O. Box 1308
Jackson, NJ 08527

VERMONT BEAN SEED CO.
Garden Lane
Fair Haven, VT 05743

SOCIETIES AND ORGANIZATIONS

AMERICAN FUCHSIA SOCIETY
County Fair Building
9th Avenue at Lincoln Way
San Francisco, CA 94122

CALIFORNIA HORTICULTURAL SOCIETY
Mrs. Elsie Mueller
1847 34th Avenue
San Francisco, CA 94122

COTTAGE GARDEN SOCIETY
Mrs. C. Tordoff
5 Nixon Close, Thornhill
Dewsbury, W. Yorkshire WF12 0JA
England

THE FLOWER AND HERB EXCHANGE
Rural Route 3, Box 239
Decorah, IA 52101

INSTITUTE FOR HISTORIC HORTICULTURE
150 White Plains Road
Tarrytown, NY 10591

INTERNATIONAL GERANIUM SOCIETY
4610 Druid Street
Los Angeles, CA 90032-3202

NATIONAL AGRICULTURAL SOCIETY
Special Collections
10301 Baltimore Boulevard
Beltsville, MD 20705

NATIONAL FUCHSIA SOCIETY
11507 E. 187th Street
Artesia, CA 90701

NEW ENGLAND GARDEN HISTORY SOCIETY
Walter Punch, Librarian MHS
300 Massachusetts Avenue
Boston, MA 02115

NORTHWEST FUCHSIA SOCIETY
Joan Hampton
P.O. Box 33071
Seattle, WA 98133-0071

SAN DIEGO HISTORICAL SOCIETY
Horticultural Heritage Society
P.O. Box 81825
San Diego, CA 92138

SEED SAVERS EXCHANGE
% Kent Whealy
Rural Route 3, Box 239
Decorah, IA 52101

SOUTHERN GARDEN HISTORY SOCIETY
Mrs. Zachary T. Bynum, Jr.
Old Salem, Inc.
Box F, Salem Station
Winston-Salem, NC 27101

THE THOMAS JEFFERSON CENTER
    FOR HISTORICAL PLANTS
Monticello
P.O. Box 316
Charlottesville, VA 22902

BIBLIOGRAPHY

Addison, Josephine. *The Illustrated Plant Lore.* London: Sidgwick & Jackson Ltd., 1985.

Allan, Mea. *Plants That Changed Our Gardens.* London: David & Charles Ltd., 1974.

Boland, Maureen and Bridget Boland. *Old Wives' Lore for Gardeners.* London: The Bodley Head Ltd., 1976.

Bourne, Hermon. *Flores Poetici: The Florist's Manual.* Boston: Munroe and Francis, 1833. Facsimile edition. Guilford, Conn.: OPUS Publications, Inc., 1988.

Breck, Joseph. *The Young Florist.* Boston: Russell Odione, 1833. Facsimile edition. Guilford, Conn.: OPUS Publications, Inc., 1988.

Clark, Jill R. *Fuchsias.* Chester, Conn.: The Globe Pequot Press, 1988.

Coats, Alice M. *Flowers and their Histories.* London: Hulton Press, Ltd., 1956.

Coats, Alice M. *The Plant Hunters.* New York: McGraw-Hill Book Co., 1969.

Coats, Alice M. *The Treasury of Flowers.* New York: McGraw-Hill Book Co., 1975.

Coombes, Allen J. *Dictionary of Plant Names.* Beaverton, Ore.: Timber Press, 1985.

Crockett, James Underwood. *Annuals.* Alexandria, Va.: Time-Life Books Inc., 1971.

Dutton, Joan Perry. *The Flower World of Williamsburg.* Williamsburg, Va.: Colonial Williamsburg, Inc., 1962.

Earle, Alice Morse. *Old Time Gardens.* New York: The Macmillan Co., 1901.

Earle, Mrs. C. W. *Pot-pourri from a Surrey Garden.* London: Smith, Elder, & Co., 1897.

Everett, Thomas H. *The New York Botanical Garden Illustrated Encyclopedia of Horticulture.* New York: Garland Publishing Inc., 1981.

Fisher, John. *Mr. Marshal's Flower Album.* London: Victor Gollancz Ltd., 1985.

Genders, Roy. *The Cottage Garden and the Old-Fashioned Flowers.* London: Pelham Books Ltd., 1969.

Harvey, John. *Early Nurserymen.* London: Phillimore & Co. Ltd., 1974.

Henderson, Peter. *Henderson's Handbook of Plants.* Jersey City: Peter Henderson & Co., 1890.

Hunn, C.E. and Bailey, L.H. *The Practical Garden Book.* New York: Grosset & Dunlap, 1906.

Index kewensis Supplement 14 (1961–65). Oxford: Oxford University Press, 1970.

Jekyll, Gertrude. *Annuals and Biennials.* London: Country Life, Ltd., 1916.

John, Humphrey. *The Skeptical Gardener.* London: George G. Harrap & Co. Ltd., 1940.

Mansfield, T.C. *Annuals in Colour and Cultivation.* London: Collins, 1949.

Martin, Laura C. *Garden Flower Folklore.* Chester, Conn.: The Globe Pequot Press, 1987.

Nehrling, Arno and Irene Nehrling. *The Picture Book of Annuals.* New York: Hearthside Press, Inc., 1966.

Newcomb, Peggy Cornett. *Popular Annuals of Eastern North America 1865–1914*. Washington, D.C.: Dumbarton Oaks, 1985.

Polunin, Oleg. *Collins Photoguide to Wild Flowers of Britain and Northern Europe*. London: William Collins Sons & Co. Ltd., 1988.

Powell, Claire. *The Meaning of Flowers*. Boulder, Co.: Shambhala Publications, Inc., 1979.

Prucha, Jaroslav. *Flowers from Seed*. New York: The Hamlyn Publishing Group, Ltd., 1977.

The Reader's Digest Association Limited. *Wild Flowers of Britain*. London: The Reader's Digest Association Limited, 1981.

Scourse, Nicolette. *The Victorians and Their Flowers*. Portland, Ore.: Timber Press, 1983.

Skinner, Charles M. *Myths and Legends of Flowers, Trees, Fruits, and Plants*. Philadelphia: J. B. Lippincott Co., 1911.

Stiff, Ruth L. A. *Flowers from the Royal Gardens of Kew*. Hanover, N. H. and London: University Press of New England, 1988.

Stuart, David. *The Garden Triumphant*. New York: Harper and Row, 1988.

Taylor, Geoffrey. *The Victorian Flower Garden*. London: Skeffington, 1952.

Vickery, Roy, ed. *Plant-Lore Studies*. London: The Folklore Society, 1984.

Waters, Michael. *The Garden in Victorian Literature*. Aldershot, U.K.: Scolar Press, 1988.

INDEX

Page numbers in italic indicate illustrations.